PRACTICAL
CHESS
EXERCISES

600 Lessons from Tactics to Strategy

Ray Cheng

wheat|mark™

Practical Chess Exercises

600 Lessons from Tactics to Strategy

Copyright © 2007 Ray Cheng. All rights reserved. No part of this book may be reproduced or retransmitted in any form or by any means without the written permission of the publisher.

Published by Wheatmark™
610 East Delano Street, Suite 104, Tucson, Arizona 85705 U.S.A.
www.wheatmark.com

ISBN: 978-1-58736-801-1
LCCN: 2007922148

Contents

Symbols

+	check
x	capture
!!	excellent move
!	good move
!?	interesting move
?!	dubious move
?	bad move
??	blunder
(D)	see corresponding diagram

*	easy
**	medium
***	difficult
****	very difficult

Foreword

Ray Cheng loves chess. I know this because he has been my student for several years and his enthusiasm has never waned. Nevertheless, when Ray first mentioned that he wanted to write a book of training exercises for the amateur player, I was skeptical. The chess market has its share of training material, including an abundance of books with collections of positions to be solved. But as Ray unfolded the plans for his work, I became more and more intrigued. He had come up with several innovative ideas, methods that offer the reader a genuine opportunity to acquire the skills needed for *actual* play.

First, instead of sorting the problems by themes, he mixes them together so that the student has no advance idea of what kind of position he is dealing with. Is there a simple checkmate, a complex tactical sequence, or a purely strategic solution to the position? Or perhaps a mixture of these elements and particular themes? With hindsight, Ray's point is obvious: this is precisely the situation that a player is confronted with in a real game! When considering your next move, you're on your own and have to decide what to play based upon your own unassisted thought process. Astonishingly, I can think of no other book that poses its problems in this way without hints about how to proceed. For example, books that ask you to find a checkmate in one, two, or three moves telegraph their intentions, whereas even books that ask 'What's the best move?' tip you off about the relevant themes and choices. By contrast, Ray's book forces you to do the most important thing of all: think for yourself.

A related problem is the degree of difficulty. Most exercise books move from easier problems to more challenging ones. Others explicitly indicate to the reader how hard a given position is to solve. Once again, this is not information imparted to a player in the real world of competition. Therefore Ray has done what seems obvious in retrospect: he has not only chosen a wide range of problems from elementary to advanced, but has randomized the order of the exercises with respect to their complexity and ease of solution. Again, this simple arrangement of material is seldom if ever to be found in other chess books.

These innovations apart, what about the problems themselves? Ray spent over a year compiling examples, drawing in large part from an unconventional source: the games of amateurs. These were typically played on the Internet, where I venture to say that the majority of games by serious players will soon be contested. Those involved in playing games via the Internet should gain insight into their typical tendencies and shortcomings. They are not so different from the ones that show up during over-the-board play, and only applied study can adequately address and correct them. Ray's understanding of the ways in which amateurs think allows him to touch upon areas of misunderstanding and oversight that don't occur to the masters who usually write exercise books. In most cases they toss together tactical examples from master games, without particular thought to the amateur audience. There could hardly be a greater contrast to the effort that Ray has invested in the book before you.

Chess authors are constantly claiming that they don't merely impart information, but also teach you how to think. As a teacher, I am painfully aware of how seldom that is the case. Truly making one's own decisions without depending upon others' advice is usually the last step in becoming a strong player. But if you carefully work through the book before you, you will inevitably improve in that regard, and gain the satisfaction that comes from greater mastery of the game.

John Watson
International Master

Introduction

This book is a training and improvement program for amateur chess players. It comprises 600 chess exercises and their solutions. It is unlike any other chess training book. While others focus only on tactics, this one covers

- Tactics
- Attack
- Defense
- Threat Identification
- Counterplay
- Openings
- Middlegames
- Endgames
- The Thought Process
- Positional Play
- Strategy

Each exercise consists of a diagrammed chess position, and your task is to find the best move. For each position you are told only which side is to move; there is no further set-up. For example, you will not find a caption under the diagram such as "White to mate in 3," or "How can Black exploit the undefended rook on a1?" The intention is to furnish only the information that you would have during a real game, when no such hints are expected or permitted. Indeed, any kind of training tends to be more effective to the extent that it simulates the conditions of actual competition. That is one of the core principles of this book. For similar reasons, the exercise positions are not grouped by theme or labeled by level of difficulty. Again, the idea is that in a real game, no one is going to whisper in your ear "Hey, you have a killer knight fork," or "You'd better spend a little extra time on this move, because it rates four stars in difficulty."

Most chess puzzle books consist entirely of tactical exercises, but there is a downside to this. Knowing at the outset that there is a tactic to be found dilutes the value of the exercise. Indeed, it encourages the reader to adopt an abridged thought process – jumping right into calculating outrageous sacrifices, for instance, without being led toward the solution by skillfully reading the clues in the position. Just as often, this reader might prematurely stop calculating once a plausible tactic has been found (and affirmed by the solution in the back of the book), without bothering to double-check whether it really works. For that reason I included a number of positions where there is a tempting tactical try that fails for some reason, and the best move is something else entirely. In real life, many (and perhaps most) tactical possibilities turn out to be flawed, and thus the habit of double-checking them is well worth cultivating. Likewise, I included positions in which it is your opponent who has the tactical threat; your job is then to identify the threat and take any appropriate defensive measures.

Many of the exercises in this book cover tactical themes, while others need not have a tactical resolution at all. There are exercises built upon positional ideas, such as outposts, weak squares, pawn structure, superior minor piece, and positional sacrifices. Other exercises are concerned with basic theoretical endgames that every chess player should know, or they feature interesting endgame positions that have occurred in practice. Many of them will illustrate important endgame concepts, including the active king, opposition, rooks behind passed pawns, and the outside passed pawn. As far as openings go, you will not be tested for your specific knowledge of theoretical "book" moves. You will, however, need to handle opening positions based on fundamental principles, such as those concerning the center, development, and castling. Of course, there will also be opening tactics and blunders to contend with.

The exercises in this book appear in random order, not only by theme, but also by level of difficulty. After all, being able to judge how much time and energy to devote to a particular position is a valuable skill during actual competition. The exercises range from very simple to very difficult, with most falling into the middle categories. For the sake of reference I have labeled the solutions (but not the exercise positions themselves, of course) with up to four stars to indicate their approximate difficulty.

Because they are not accompanied by artificial hints, working through these exercises will instill a more complete and realistic move selection process. They present opportunities to utilize and strengthen your tactical vision, positional understanding, theoretical knowledge, and intuitive judgment in an integrated and holistic manner. In addition, they will enhance your ability to anticipate your opponent's ideas, calculate variations, and evaluate the resulting positions accurately.

Consistent with the spirit of this book, you should try to solve each problem directly from the diagram; or, set up the initial position on a board, but do all of the analysis in your head without moving the pieces. You can even use a clock to add the time element, giving yourself, say, half an hour to do each page of six positions. In short, these exercises will help you to develop the full range of skills that you need to succeed in practical play. Unlike a real game, however, you will receive immediate, constructive feedback on every move selection. In addition, these exercises will put you in contact with a wealth of important chess themes and ideas, not all of which you may have encountered in your own games.

The solutions were checked using a number of strong computer engines. The main line of each solution appears in **bold** face. Sometimes the main line follows not the objectively best defense, but rather the "greatest plausible resistance." For example, the best defense to a tactical combination might be to accede to the loss of a knight on move two; however, by putting up reasonable resistance the defender might last five additional moves, and then lose a rook. This approach helps to bring out relevant variations, and more closely corresponds to the way most humans think. In some exercises, particularly those with a strategic or positional theme, there is necessarily a subjective element. While in those cases there may be more than one acceptable move, I tried to select one that would meet the requirements of the position in a special way.

Finally, this collection of exercises is distinguished by another critical feature: the vast majority of the positions were taken from amateur games. (I relied on master games primarily for examples of positional play.) Why should this make a difference? We amateurs use a much wider variety of openings than masters, many considered unsound at the highest levels (and indeed some are unsound at any level!). We rightfully continue playing out positions that the professional would dismiss as resignable. We make more mistakes; we make worse mistakes; and we make mistakes of different kinds. Positions arising from master games can be marvels of piece coordination and activity. In our games, however, it is not uncommon for both players to have placed their pieces awkwardly, or to have pursued plans inconsistent with the demands of the position. Rudolf Spielmann once quipped, "I can see Alekhine's combinations as well as he can, I just can't get his positions." Spielmann was a world class master; his words should place into perspective the difficulties the rest of us suffer down in the lower sections.

For all these reasons, the positions you will find on the following pages do not resemble those gathered in other chess exercise books. Rather, they contain the full range of challenges and opportunities that we ordinary mortals face at the chessboard, on the long road toward improvement and success.

Exercises and Solutions

The following pages contain 600 chess training exercises. Each exercise consists of a diagrammed chess position. You are told only which side has the move. For each position your task is to find the best move, and be able to support your choice using words and analysis.

The exercises are laid out on the left-hand pages, six to a page. Their solutions appear on the corresponding right-hand pages (rather than a separate section at the end of the book). The solutions should be covered up using a large index card or a folded sheet of paper, and uncovered as you proceed through the exercises.

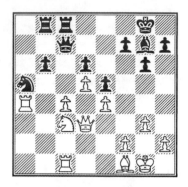

1. Black to move

4. White to move

2. White to move

5. White to move

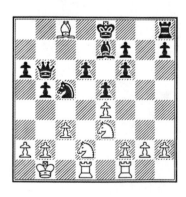

3. Black to move

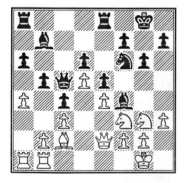

6. White to move

(1)* Fork
1...Nb3! 2.Rb1 Nc5 wins the exchange (i.e., a rook for a minor piece).

(2)** Trapped piece, look for better move
White could certainly pick up the exchange by 1.Bxd8. But with so few open files, and with so many pieces on the board, the material imbalance might not be advantageous for quite some time. Besides, White should first check whether there is an even better move, and indeed there is one: **1.Nb4!** traps the Black queen. (1.Nd4 is also effective.) Note that the desperate try 1...Nxe4 would be met by 2.Qe3.

(3)*** Deny enemy outposts
There isn't a tactical shot, but there is a positional crisis. Given the chance, White would play Nd5 and Bf5, when his finely placed pieces can stand up to Black's queen. Black stops this plan by **1...Ne6!**. Now **2.Nd5** runs into **2...Qc6 3.Bxe6 fxe6** driving the piece back.

(4)*** Gain a crucial tempo
White's plan is to abandon the b-pawn, and rush his king over to the kingside to eat Black's remaining pawns. He gains a precious tempo with this little finesse: **1.Kb2!! Kb5 2.Kc3 Kc5 3.Kd3 Kb4 4.Ke4 Kxb3**. The point is that the White king is on e4 rather than d3 when Black captures the b-pawn. As it turns out, this one tempo makes the difference between a win and a draw.

(5)** Remove the guard, skewer
White wins heavy material by **1.Qxg5!**, removing the defender of h7: **1...fxg5 2.Rh8+ Kf7 3.R8h7+ Kg8 4.Rxc7**.

(6)* Blunder check
The White knight on g3 is hanging (since the f2 pawn is pinned). Moving it away is best: **1.Nf1**.

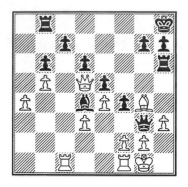

7. Black to move

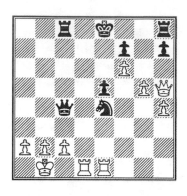

10. Black to move

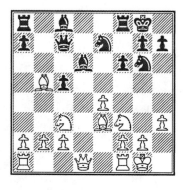

8. White to move

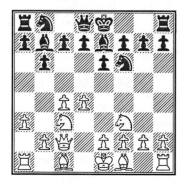

11. White to move

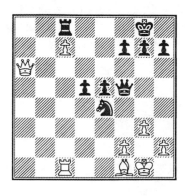

9. White to move

12. White to move

(7)** Deflection, mate
After **1...f3!** (threatening mate and deflecting the defender of h3) **2.Bxf3 Rxh3**, White cannot prevent mate.

(8)** Clearance, fork
1.Bc4+ (clearing b5 for the knight) **1...Kh8 2.Nb5** scoops up the bishop on d6.

(9)** Deflection, promotion
1.Qxc8+! Qxc8 2.Ba6!. Black must give up his queen or allow the pawn to promote.

(10)**** Piece sacrifice to expose enemy king
The obvious try **1...Qxc2+ 2.Ka1 Rb8 3.Qe2 Qxe2 4.Rxe2 Nc5 5.Rxe5+ Ne6** leads to an unclear struggle. Instead, Black can take charge with the spectacular piece sac **1...Nc3+!! 2.bxc3 Qxc3 3.Qe2** [3.Re2 Rb8+ 4.Kc1 Qa1+ 5.Kd2 Rd8+ nabs a rook; 3.a3 Qxc2+ 4.Ka1 Qc3+ 5.Ka2 Ra8 and White must shed a rook via 6.Rxe5+ to stave off immediate mate] **3...Rb8+ 4.Kc1 Qa3+ 5.Kd2 Rd8**. White must give up his queen.

(11)** Obtain ideal pawn center
Black has taken a pause from the struggle to control the e4 square, so White should seize the ideal pawn center by **1.e4!.**

(12)** Achieve opposite-colored bishops
Down two pawns, White's best chance to hold a draw is **1.Bg5! Ke6 2.Bxf6 Bxf6**, reaching an ending with opposite-colored bishops. White can hope to set up a blockade along the light squares.

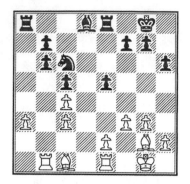

13. Black to move

16. White to move

14. White to move

17. White to move

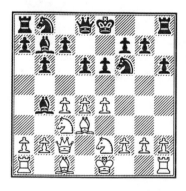

15. White to move

18. White to move

(13)*** Positional pawn sac
1...e4! 2.fxe4 Ne5. Black gets an outpost for his knight, the e-file (with targets) for his rook, and greater scope for his bishop. White's light-squared bishop is obstructed by his own pawn on e4, however.

(14)*** Swap defender of outposts
To take advantage of the nice squares at c4, d6 and f5, White has **1.Bc4!**, eliminating the enemy sentry. **1...Bxc4** [or 1...Bf8 2.Bxf7+ Kxf7 3.Qc4+ Kg7 4.Nf1 followed by Nf1-g3-f5] **2.Qxc4+ Kf8 3.Qe6**. Now White can plan on Nd2-c4-d6.

(15)* Fork, pin
1.Qa4+ wins a piece, as **1...Nc6** is met by **2.d5**.

(16)*** The tactic fails!
White would maintain his clear advantage after the sensible **1.Rf1** or **1.Qe2**. The tactical shot 1.Rxg7+? is tempting, and should be looked at, but 1...Kxg7 2.Bh6+ Kh8 3.Qg5? (expecting 3...f5 4.Qxh4 with compensation) loses to 3...Nf3+! 4.gxf3 Rg8 winning the White queen.

(17)*** Saved by stalemate or perpetual check
The White king is sequestered at a8, preventing the a-pawn from promoting. On the other hand, the Black pawns have a clearer path toward the first rank. White escapes with a half point by **1.Ra5+ Kh4** [1...Kf6 2.Rf5+!] **2.Rh5+! Kg3 3.Rh3+! Kxh3** stalemate.

(18)** Strategic pawn maneuver
White must act quickly to engage the enemy before the latter catches up in development. One way forward is **1.a4!**. Now if **1...b4** [1...bxa4 2.Rxa4 Be7 3.Nd2 intending Nc4 with the advantage; on 1...Rb8 2.axb5 axb5 3.Ra7 White seizes the 7th rank] **2.Rac1 Be7 3.b3** then White has a target at c5, an outpost at c4, a share of the open file, and a kingside pawn majority.

19. White to move

22. Black to move

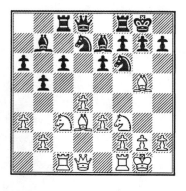

20. White to move

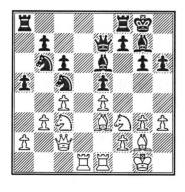

23. White to move

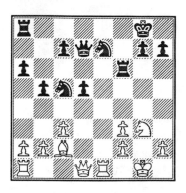

21. White to move

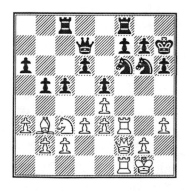

24. White to move

(19)* Back rank weakness
1.Qc8+ Qxc8 [1...Ne8 2.Qxb8] **2.Rxc8+ Ne8 3.Rxe8** mate.

(20)** Stop thematic pawn advance
Black's counterplay in the Semi-Slav Defense relies on the ...c6-c5 advance, opening the diagonal for his light-squared bishop, extending the scope of the rook on c8, and challenging White's pawn center. Here, after unusually restrained play by both sides, White can prevent Black's thematic advance by **1.b4!**.

(21)* Overworked piece, double attack
1.Rxe7! wins a piece, as after **1...Qxe7 2.Qxd5+** White snags the d-pawn and the loose rook on a8.

(22)** Rook and pawn endgame
Black will eventually have to give up his rook for the c-pawn. His hopes rest with his remaining pawn on a6. **1...Rc4!** is the winning move, allowing the king to join the struggle via c3. [1...Rxc7? is premature as 2.Kxc7 Kc4 3.Kb6 is a draw; 1...Rc2? doesn't allow the Black king to penetrate in time 2.Kd7 Kd5 3.c8Q Rxc8 4.Kxc8 Kc6 5.Kb8, with a draw] **2.Kd7 Kc3 3.c8Q Rxc8 4.Kxc8 Kxb4** winning.

(23)*** Double attack, pin
1.Qc1! wins the Black h-pawn. If Black tries to defend it by **1...Kh7?**, then White wins yet more material by **2.Qa3 Nbd7 3.Na4**.

(24)** Positional exchange sac
1.Rxf6! gxf6 2.Nd5 Qd8 3.Nxf6+ Kg7 4.Bd5. For the exchange, White gets a pawn; sole ownership of the d5 outpost; greater control of the squares f5, f6 and h5; heavy pressure down the f-file; and a weakened enemy king.

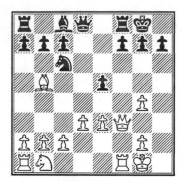

25. Black to move

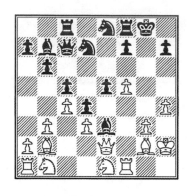

28. Black to move

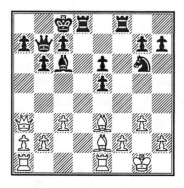

26. Black to move

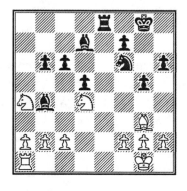

29. Black to move

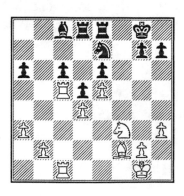

27. White to move

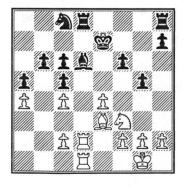

30. White to move

(25)** Fork, double attack
1...Nd4! 2.exd4 Qxd4+ 3.Kh2 Qxb2. Black regains his piece, remaining two pawns up.

(26)* Prevent deadly pin
Black's first order of business is to prevent Ba6, losing his queen. Thus **1...Kb8**.

(27)** Superior minor piece
1.Bh4! Bb7 2.Bxe7 Rxe7. White removes a defender of the backward pawn at c6, and is left with the superior minor piece.

(28)*** Pawn sac to open lines
1...e4! 2.Bxe4 Bxe4 3.dxe4. In return for the pawn, Black has cleared e5 for a knight, the e-file for his rooks, and the b8–h2 diagonal for his queen. There followed **3...Nef6 4.Ng2 Rfe8 5.Nd2** [5.Nxe3 would be answered by 5...Rxe4] **5...Bxd2 6.Qxd2 Qxg3+! 7.Kxg3 Nxe4+ 8.Kf4 Nxd2**. Black has emerged with an extra advanced, protected passed pawn. (Polugaevsky – Petrosian, Moscow 1970)

(29)* Discovered attack
1...c5 picks up one of the loose White knights.

(30)*** Rook and pawn(s) vs. bishop and knight
Whether a rook and pawn(s) are worth more than two minor pieces depends on the activity level of the remaining pieces (including pawns). Here, after **1.Nxg5! fxg5 2.Bxg5+ Ke6 3.Bxd8 Rxd8 4.f4 Rf8 5.e5 Be7 6.g3**, White has a mobile passed pawn mass and his rooks control the d-file; Black's pieces, in contrast, do not have decent squares.

31. Black to move

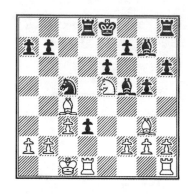

34. Black to move

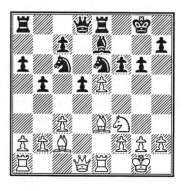

32. White to move

35. White to move

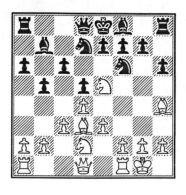

33. White to move

36. Black to move

(31)** *Zugzwang*

White's king cannot be forced away from the corner, but his pawns can be forced to abandon their sovereign. Here is one way to do it: **1...Bc2 2.Ka2 Bb1+ 3.Ka1 Kc2** White is in *zugzwang* – he is compelled to make a move to his disadvantage! **4.b3 axb3 5.a4 b2** mate.

(32)** Double attack, discovered attack

1.Bb3! is decisive: **1...Rb8** [1...Kh8 2.Qxd5 wins one of the knights; 1...Nxe5 2.Bxd5 with a double attack on a8 and e6] **2.Bxd5 Qd7 3.exf6 Bxf6 4.Bg5** with the double threat of Bxe6+ and Bxf6.

(33)** Prevent opponent from castling

White already stands much better, and he can compound his opponent's misery by **1.Ng6!**, for after 1...Rg8 [not **1...fxg6?? 2.Bxg6** mate] Black is denied the right to castle short.

(34)** Decoy, fork, remove the guard

1...d2+! 2.Rxd2 Rxd2 3.Kxd2 Ne4+ 4.Ke3 Nxg3 5.hxg3 Bxe5 wins a piece.

(35)** Down a piece, swap pawns

White's best chance to salvage a draw is **1.c5!**, forcing the exchange of Black's last pawn. 1.d4? would allow Black to create a passed pawn: 1...Rg1 2.c5 Rb1+ 3.Kc4 b5+, winning.

(36)* Skewer

1...Bh6! skewers the White queen to the undefended bishop on c1.

37. White to move

40. White to move

38. Black to move

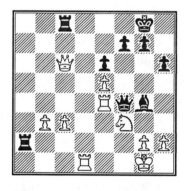

41. Black to move

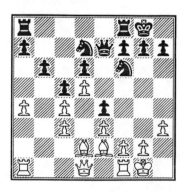

39. Black to move

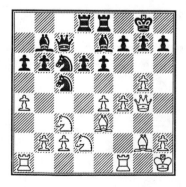

42. Black to move

(37)* Mate
1.Rb8+ Bf8 2.Bh6 with mate to follow.

(38)* Domination
1...Bd5! immobilizes the White knight. With the White king likewise chained to b3, Black will now attack the kingside.

(39)** Prevent opponent's plan
White could try to create a weakness at a7 or b6 by means of an a4-a5 advance. **17...a5!** prevents this idea. The backward pawn at b6 is easily defended.

(40)**** My horse for your kingdom
The g5 knight is needed to cover the f7 flight square – but only for one more tempo: **1.Nh4+!! Kxg5** [1...Kh5 2.Rh8+ Kxg5 (2...Kg4 3.h3+ Kxg5 4.f4 mate) 3.f4+ Kg4 4.h3 mate; 1...Kh6 2.Rh8+ Kxg5 3.f4+ Kg4 4.h3 mate] **2.f4+ Kh5** [2...Kg4 3.h3+ Kh5 4.Rh8 mate; 2...Kh6 3.Rh8 mate] **3.Rh8+ Kg4 4.h3** mate.

(41)*** Rescue attacked queen
Both queens are *en prise* (i.e., subject to capture). After the simple exchange 1...Rxc6? 2.Rxf4, White would stand better due to his connected passed pawns. Does Black have anything better? He should look for a way to get his queen to a safe square with check, investing some material if necessary. Here's the way: **1...Rxg2+! 2.Kh1** [or 2.Kxg2 Qxf3+ 3.Kg1 Qxd1+ 4.Kf2 Rxc6] **2...Rxh2+! 3.Nxh2 Bf3+ 4.Nxf3 Qxf3+ 5.Kh2 Rxc6** with a winning material advantage.

(42)*** Meet flank attack with central action
White has an impressive build-up on the kingside. However, Black can effectively counter with a central thrust. **1...Nb4! 2.Rac1 d5! 3.exd5 Nxd5 4.Nxd5 Bxd5.** Now Black has active pieces, the last remaining center pawn, and the more secure king.

43. White to move

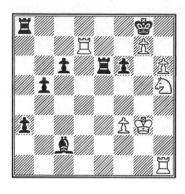

46. White to move

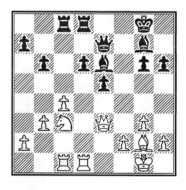

44. White to move

47. Black to move

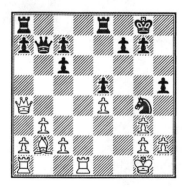

45. White to move

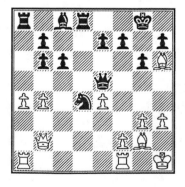

48. Black to move

(43)* Stalemate
White escapes with a draw by **1.b8Q+! Qxb8** stalemate.

(44)** Eliminate defender of outpost
1.Bd5! eliminates the last Black minor piece defending d5. **1...Kh7 2.Bxe6 Qxe6 3.Rd3 Rc7 4.Rcd1 Rf7 5.Ne4** (concentrating his forces on the backward pawn) **5...Bf8 6.Rd5**. White soon won the d6 pawn and the game. (Smyslov – Denker, USA/USSR Radio Match 1946)

(45)*** Parry deadly threat
White had better contend with **1...Qb6+!** when the first player must shed material at d4, or succumb to "Philidor's Legacy," **2.Kh1 Nf2+ 3.Kg1 Nh3+ 4.Kh1 Qg1+ 5.Rxg1 Nf2** mate. **1.Qa5** is best, preventing the initial check. Note that **1.Rd2??** loses to **1...Qb6+ 2.Kf1 Qe3!** with the fatal threat of ...Nxh2 mate.

(46)**** Deflection
Note that Black's e6 rook defends against Nxf6 mate. Now **1.Re1!** either deflects or wins this crucial piece. **1...Rac8** [or **1...a2 2.Rxe6 a1Q 3.Nxf6+ Qxf6 4.Rxf6** and wins; **1...Bg6 2.Rxe6 Bxh5 3.Rxf6 a2 4.Rf8+ Rxf8 5.h7+ Kxh7 6.gxf8Q+** mating] **2.Nxf6+ Rxf6 3.Rxe8+ Kh7 4.Rh8+ Kg6 5.g8Q+** with mate to follow.

(47)** Double attack
1...Rxc1+ 2.Qxc1 Qe2. The double attack on f3 and f2 is decisive.

(48)* Double attack
1...Bxh3! 2.Bxh3 Qh5. Black regains the piece and emerges an additional pawn ahead.

49. Black to move

52. Black to move

50. Black to move

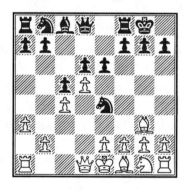

53. Black to move

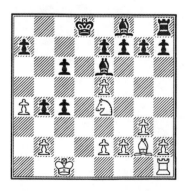

51. White to move

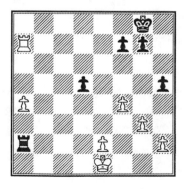

54. White to move

(49)** Double attack, pin, weak back rank
Black wins material by **1...Qd8!** (attacking h4 and d2) [1...Rad8 2.Rc2 Bf5 3.Rb2 Bxb1 also wins] **2.Qxd8+ Raxd8 3.Rc2 Bb3**.

(50)*** Discovered check, mate
1...Rc2+ 2.Kb1 Be4! 3.Rc1 [or 3.Rg1 (otherwise, White loses his rook to the discovered check) Rxc3! 4.Ka1 Rxc3] **3...Rb2+ 4.Ka1 Ra2** mate.

(51)*** Imprison enemy piece
1.Ng5!! Kc7 [1...Kd7 2.Rd1+ Kc7 3.Nxe6+ fxe6 is similar to the game] **2.Nxe6+ fxe6 3.h4 g6 4.f4** and the Black bishop will never see the light of day. (Miles – Smyslov, Dortmund 1986)

(52)*** Clearance, blockade
1...f2!! clears the f3 square for the bishop [1...Be8? loses due to 2.g6+ Kh6 3.Ke6!] **2.Bxf2 Bf3 3.h6 Kg6**. Black has successfully blockaded the enemy passed pawns, ensuring a draw.

(53)** Weak diagonal
Black wins two pawns by **1...Qa5+ 2.b4 cxb4 3.Bf4** (to cover d2) **3...bxa3+ 4.Bd2 Qb6** (threatening ...Qxf2 mate) **5.e3 Qb2**.

(54)**** Restrict enemy king
Black would like to play ...g7-g6, followed by ...Kg8-g7-f6. After **1.f5!!** it is much more difficult for Black to activate his king. (Kramnik – Timman, Wijk aan Zee 1999)

55. White to move

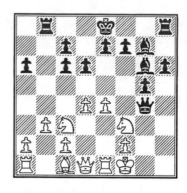

58. Black to move

56. White to move

59. Black to move

57. Black to move

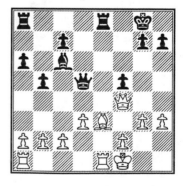

60. Black to move

(55)* Rook behind passed pawn

Rooks generally belong behind passed pawns, and that is the case here: **1.Rd1!** followed by **2.Ra1** gives White the best winning chances.

(56)*** Exchange opponent's best piece

1.Rd1! forces the trade of Black's only developed piece. **1...Rxd1** [1...Rc7 2.Rc5 Rb7 3.Rc8! threatening Rdd8 and Bc5(+)] **2.Kxd1** and now **2...Kd7 3.Rb8!** keeps Black's pieces tied down for several more moves. (Fischer – Euwe, Leipzig 1960)

(57)* Fork

Black picks up the vulnerable d3 bishop by **1...Nc5 2.Qc2 Nb4**.

(58)* Pin

1...Qh3+! 2.Ke2 [or 2.Kg1 g4] **2...g4**. Black wins back a piece (as the c3 knight is unprotected) and continues the onslaught.

(59)** Improve piece placement

1...Nd7!. The knight is heading for e6, where it will harass the d4 pawn and support his kingside pawn advance [1...Ne8 is less effective due to 2.Bf4]. **2.Kf1 Nf8 3.Ke2 Ne6**. (Saidy – Fischer, New York 1964)

(60)** Pin, skewer, mate

1...Rxe3! 2.Qxe3 [2.Rxe3 Qh1+ 3.Ke2 Qxa1 Black remains a piece to the good; 2.fxe3 Qg2 mate] **2...Qg2+ 3.Ke2 Re8**. Black gets a decisive material advantage.

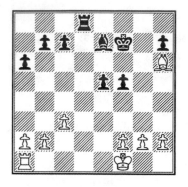

61. White to move

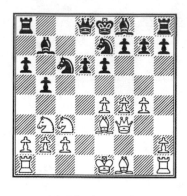

64. Black to move

62. Black to move

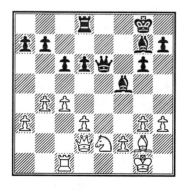

65. White to move

63. Black to move

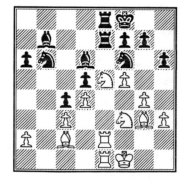

66. White to move

(61)*** Create safe retreat
The h6 bishop is fast running out of safe squares. For instance, 1.Be3? f4 leaves White with the unpleasant choice between 2.Ba7 b6 when his bishop is out of play, or 2.Bc1 Rd1+ 3.Ke2 Rg1 when his rook is snookered. White can remedy the situation by either **1.g3** securing the e3 square, or **1.Re1** gaining a tempo and clearing c1 for a safe retreat.

(62)** Skewer, remove the guard
Black wins material by **1...Rxf3+ 2.Kxf3 Bxe4+** followed by **3...Bxh1**.

(63)*** Neutralize threat
1...a4 is the only move. White was threatening to play b2-b4, hitting the knight that holds back the devastating Qa6+.

(64)*** Pawn sac creates outpost
1...g5! 2.fxg5 [other moves concede e5 without pocketing the offered material, e.g., 2.0–0–0 gxf4 3.Qxf4 Ng6 4.Qg3 Nce5] **2...Ne5**. Black has created an outpost for her knight, gained a tempo by attacking the White queen, and hampered White's kingside pawn storm. (Shirov – J. Polgár, Buenos Aires 1994)

(65)* Trapped piece
1.g4! traps a bishop.

(66)* Discovered attack, fork, pin
White wins at least the exchange after **1.Ng6+! fxg6 2.Bxd6** due to the resulting pin.

67. White to move

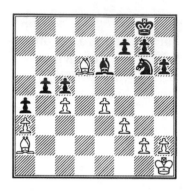

70. White to move

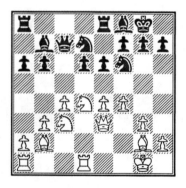

68. Black to move

71. Black to move

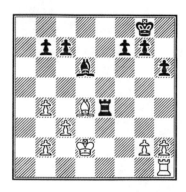

69. Black to move

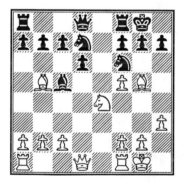

72. White to move

(67)** Pin, weak back rank
1.bxc5! [White is only up a pawn after 1.Rc1 Bxe3 2.fxe3 Kf8
3.bxc5] **1...Bxc5 2.Rc1** wins since the Black bishop is pinned
against back rank mate. Note that **2...Bb6** would simply be met
by **3.Bxb6** when Black cannot both recapture at b6 and defend
his king.

(68)*** The hedgehog unleashed
Black has adopted a "hedgehog" set-up. White enjoys more
space, but Black is solid and has potential for counterplay,
typically associated with the pawn advances ...b5 and ...e5. Here
the thematic **1...e5!** wins material: **2.Nc2** [2.fxe5? dxe5 3.Nf5
Bc5; 2.Nde2? Ng4 3.Qf3 Qc5+ 4.Kh1 Nf2+] **2...Ng4 3.Qe2
Qc5+ 4.Kf1 Nxh2+.**

(69)** Overworked piece, blunder check
The pawn at c3 is overworked, but after 1...Bxb4?? 2.Kd3 it is
Black who must lose material. The right approach is **1...Rg4!**
stepping away from the White king's reach with tempo, **2.g3** and
only now **2...Bxb4**. Black will keep the extra pawn.

(70)** Create passed pawn
1.cxb5! Bc8 [the point is that after 1...Bxa2 2.b6 the pawn
cannot be stopped; White wins the foot race 1...c4 2.b6 c3 3.b7
since he promotes with check] **2.Bxc5**. Black will have to give
up a piece for the passed pawn.

(71)** Stop threatened combination
Black must prevent 1.Nxf7! Kxf7 2.Qxe6+ Kg6 3.Bd3+ Kh5
4.Qh3 mate. Best is **1...Nb6**, lending the bishop's protection to
e6.

(72)** Pin, fork, remove the guard
White wins at least a piece by **1.Bxd7 Qxd7 2.Bxf6 Qxf5**
[2...Bb6 3.Qg4 mating soon; 2...gxf6 3.Nxf6+ winning the
queen] **3.Nxc5 dxc5 4.Bc3**.

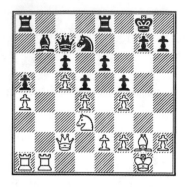

73. White to move

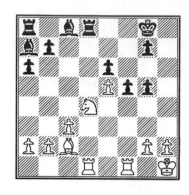

76. White to move

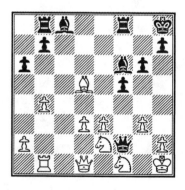

74. White to move

77. Black to move

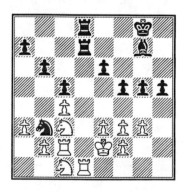

75. Black to move

78. Black to move

(73)*** Eliminate defender of key square

1.Ne5! (intending to swap off the minor piece defending b6)
1...Nxe5 2.fxe5 Reb8 3.Rb6 Ba6 4.Rab1. The rook on b6
attacks a6 and c6, it cuts off the Black queen's defense of a5, and
its exchange results in a White passed pawn. (Portisch –
Radulov, Budapest 1969)

(74)*** Trapped piece

1.Nf4! closes the lid on the enemy queen [1.Ng1? fails to 1...f4!
allowing the queen to escape]. Black's best chance now is
1...Rd8 2.Nh3 Qxf1+ 3.Qxf1 Rxd5, though White still has a
winning material advantage.

(75)**** Force strategically favorable exchanges

1...Na1!! forces the exchange of both pairs of rooks, adding
strength to the impending passed h-pawn. **2.Rxd7 Rxd7 3.Rd2
Rxd2+ 4.Kxd2 h4 5.gxh4** [on 5.Ke2 h3 6.Kf1 Bxc3 7.bxc3 Nc2
Black will pick off queenside pawns] **5...gxh4 6.N1e2 h3 7.Ng3
h2 8.f4**. With the g3 knight glued to the promotion square, Black
will play the rest of the board effectively a piece up. (Analysis
from J. Donaldson – R. Costigan, USCL Exhibition 2005)

(76)** Discovered attack, mate

1.Nxf5! uncovers an attack on d8. **1...Rxd1** [1...exf5 2.Rxd8+
Kh7 3.Bxf5+ is brutal] **2.Ne7+ Kh8 3.Rxd1 Bb6** (defending d8)
[3...g6 4.Rd8+ wins the c8 bishop] **4.Bg6!** Black must shed
heavy material or face a deadly check along the h-file.

(77)** Stave off attack

1...Nf6! parries the threat to h7 (note that the g5 pawn is pinned)
2.Qf3 Nxe4 3.dxe4 e5! 4.g6 [4.f5 Bxf5! 5.exf5?? e4] **4...exf4**.
Now Black is much better.

(78)** Pin, weak back rank

1...Qxc1+! 2.Qxc1 Rb1 3.h3 Rxc1+ 4.Kh2 Rd1 and wins.

38

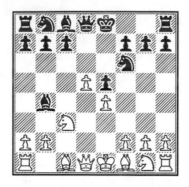

79. White to move

82. Black to move

80. White to move

83. Black to move

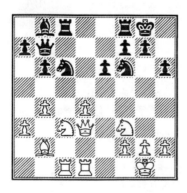

81. White to move

84. White to move

(79)* Double attack
1.Qa4+ wins a piece.

(80)**** Attack hanging pawns
The "hanging pawns" at c5 and d5 must be put under pressure.
1.Ne1! (heading to d3, to chew on c5) **1...Rbc8 2.Bg4** (to
pressure a defender of c5) **2...Qg6 3.Bh3 Rc7 4.Nd3**. White
threatens Qa5 as well as Nf4. The finish was **4...Nf6 5.Qa5 Ne8
6.Rxc5 Rxc5 7.Nxc5**. Facing heavy material loss, Black
resigned. (Korchnoi – Geller, Moscow 1971)

(81)*** Thematic advance of the IQP
One of the strategic motifs of the isolated queen pawn (IQP) is
its well-timed advance: **1.d5! exd5 2.Nxd5 Nxd5 3.Qxd5**. White
has thereby succeeded in exchanging Black's only kingside
minor piece, opening the long diagonal for his bishop, and
creating tactical opportunities based on the weakness of c6, d7
and g7. (Portisch – Browne, Amsterdam 1971)

(82)** Don't allow stalemate
Black must give the White king air to breathe, as 1...bxa5?? 2.b6
axb6 is stalemate. Instead, **1...Ke3 2.axb6 axb6 3.Kg1** wins:
Black needs only nine moves to promote a pawn, while White
would need eleven.

(83)*** Liberate piece, develop counterplay
1...e6? looks "solid," but condemns the Black bishop to
passivity. However, **1...f4!!** creates the possibility of counterplay
along the f-file, and of developing the bishop to f5, outside the
pawn chain. (Em. Lasker – Tartakower, Mährisch-Ostrau 1923)

(84)*** Mate
1.Nf7! does force checkmate, but Black's tricks have to be
checked out carefully. The end might be **1...Rg1+!** [1...Rb1
2.Rh6+ Kg4 3.Rh4 mate] **2.Kh3!** [not 2.Kxg1?? d1Q+]
2...d1N!? (threatening mate himself, just in case White has a
lapse) [or 2...Rxg3+ 3.Kxg3 d1Q 4.Rh6 mate] **3.Rh6** mate.

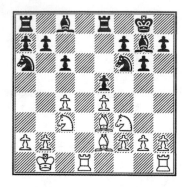

85. Black to move

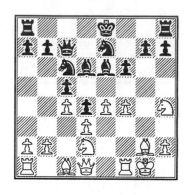

88. White to move

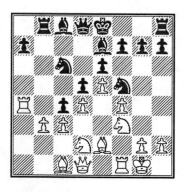

86. Black to move

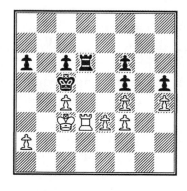

89. Black to move

87. Black to move

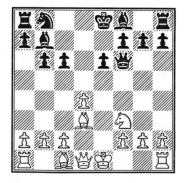

90. White to move

(85)** Swap favorably, impose doubled pawns

1...Ng4!. Black exchanges White's better bishop and inflicts doubled e-pawns. There followed **2.a3** [2.Rd3 only delays the inevitable 2...Be6 3.b3 Nb4 4.Rd2 Nxe3 5.fxe3 Bh6] **2...Nxe3 3.fxe3 Bh6** and the e3 pawn falls.

(86)* Fork

1...Ne3! wins the exchange.

(87)* Discovered attack

1...Nxd4! nets a pawn after **2.Qxd7** [or 2.Qd1 Nxf3+ 3.Nxf3] **2...Nxf3+ 3.Nxf3 Nxd7.**

(88)*** Pawn sac for piece activity

1.e5! fxe5 2.f5! Bf7 3.Ne4. For the material investment White gets the e4 square for his knight and a long diagonal for his bishop; meanwhile Black's queen-bishop battery has been sealed off by his own pawn. (Botvinnik – Pomar, Varna 1962)

(89)** Avoid rook exchange

1...Re6 is the only move, after which Black retains practical drawing chances. Trading rooks would be a mistake, since White is able to create a passed e-pawn unassisted by his king. That frees the White king to advance or to attack the Black a-pawn.

(90)* Trapped piece

1.Bg5! traps the Black queen.

91. Black to move

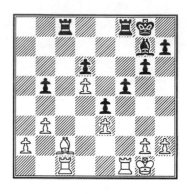

94. Black to move

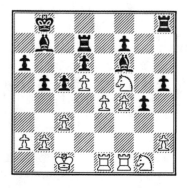

92. Black to move

95. Black to move

93. White to move

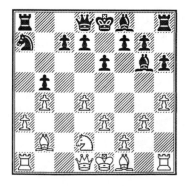

96. White to move

(91)*** Guard against perpetual check

The immediate capture 1...Rxa2? would allow perpetual check by 2.Qc8+ Kh7 3.Qh3+ Kg6 [or 3..Qh6 4.Qf5+] 4.Qf5+ etc. Better is **1...Qe4+! 2.Kg1 Qd4+ 3.Kh1 Qd5+ 4.Kg1 Qc5+ 5.Kh1 Qc6+ 6.Kg1**. Now that the Black queen covers c8 against the "perp," it's time for **6...Rxa2!**.

(92)** Remove superior enemy piece

The knight on f5 ties a Black rook to the defense of d6, and holds up Black's kingside pawn majority. Thus **1...Rdd8!** intending **2...Bc8** to swap off or swat away the enemy horse. (Bogoljubow – Alekhine, Pforzheim 1934)

(93)* Discovered attack

1.Bxd4 Bxd4 2.Bb5+ wins a piece.

(94)* Pin, remove the guard, overworked piece

Black wins a piece by hitting the defender of the c2 bishop: **1...Bb2! 2.Rb1 Rxc2**. Also good is 1...Bh6 2.Rfe1 Rc3 3.Kf2 Rfc8 4.Re2 (this rook is now overworked) 4...Bxe3+ 5.Rxe3 Rxc2+ 6.Rxc2 Rxc2+ 7.Re2 [7.Kg3 Rxa2 8.Rc3 Rd2] 7...Rxe2+ 8.Kxe2 b4 with a straightforward win.

(95)** Superior minor piece

1...Bxb4! ensures that Black is left with the superior minor piece: **2.cxb4** [2.Rxb4 b5 is no better] **2...Na3 3.Rb3 Nb5 4.e3** (another White pawn on the same color as the bishop) **4...Rc2 5.a4 Nd6**. The knight will return to the c4 outpost after the a8 rook has joined in the offensive. (Najdorf – Averbakh, Zürich 1953)

(96)*** Positional pawn sac

1.d5! exd5 2.Bg2 c6 3.0-0. The long diagonal has been opened for the b2 bishop, which bears down on g7, thus disrupting Black's kingside development. Meanwhile, the Black knight has been sidelined. (Kasparov – Andersson, Tilburg 1981)

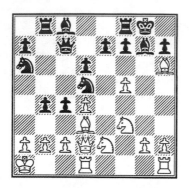

97. White to move

100. White to move

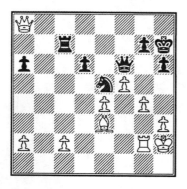

98. Black to move

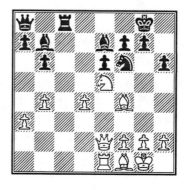

101. White to move

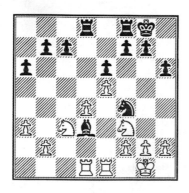

99. White to move

102. Black to move

(97)* An overriding factor
Don't worry about the attacked piece. **1.Qg5!** and it's mate next move.

(98)*** Overworked piece
1...Qh4! overworks the White rook, which cannot defend both c2 and g4. Black now threatens **2...Nf3+ 3.Kh1 Qxh3+ 4.Rh2 Qxh2** mate. There is no adequate defense: 2.Rf2 Nxg4+ 3.Kg2 Nxe3+; 2.Re2 Nxg4+ 3.Kg1 Qg3+ 4.Kf1 Nxe3+; 2.Rg3 Rxc2+ 3.Kh1 Qxg3.

(99)** Exploit loose pieces
1.g3! Nh3+ 2.Kg2 Bf5 3.Nh4 Ng5 4.Nxf5 exf5 5.d5! (to control e6) **5...Rfe8 6.f4 Nh7.** White stands much better, with more space and the superior knight.

(100)** Caught in a mating net
1.Rxg7! Rxf3 (or else 2.Rh6 is mate) **2.Kxf3 e4+ 3.Kf4 Rxg7** [3...Kxh4 4.Rh6 mate] **4.Rh6** mate.

(101)** Double attack, remove the guard
White can snatch an important pawn by **1.Nxf7!**, since **1...Kxf7? 2.Qxe6+ Kf8 3.Qxe7+ Kg8 4.Bxh6 gxh6 5.Qxf6** is a bloodbath.

(102)* *Le Trébuchet*
1...Kd2! 2.Kf4 Kd3!. White must surrender his pawn and the game.

103. White to move

106. White to move

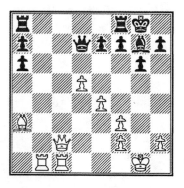

104. White to move

107. White to move

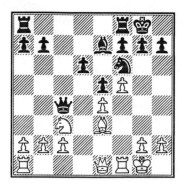

105. White to move

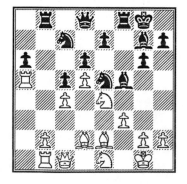

108. Black to move

(103)** Preserve fine king position

1.h5 is necessary to prevent **...g7-g5**, which would otherwise drive the White king away from its excellent position.

(104)** Seize the 7th rank

1.Qc7! is the only way forward. Anything else would allow Black to contest the c-file with a rook. The continuation was **1...Qh3!** [1...Qxc7 2.Rxc7 and e7 falls] **2.Qg3!** (denying any counterplay) **2...Qxg3+** [2...Qd7? 3.Rc7 Qa4 4.Bxe7] **3.hxg3 Rfe8 4.Rb7 Bf8 5.Rcc7.** White is in complete command. (Gelfand – Kindermann, Dortmund 1990)

(105)*** The mother of all outposts

White would like to post his knight on the magnificent d5 square. Thus **1.Bg5!** to remove the last minor piece that can challenge d5. **1...Rfe8 2.Bxf6 Bxf6 3.Nd5!.** White's minor piece is better by far. Now Black must avoid **3...Qxc2** as he would lose the exchange by **4.Rf2 Qc6 5.Rc1 Qa4 6.b3 Qd7 7.Nc7.** (Smyslov – Rudakovsky, Moscow 1945)

(106)*** Take control of open file

1.Rc6! leaves Black with the unpleasant choice between **1...Rxc6** [not 1...Nb8 2.Rxc8+ Qxc8 3.Rc1 Qd8 4.Qc4 penetrating decisively] **2.dxc6 Qe6** [2...Qxc6?? 3.b5] giving White a protected passed pawn, or allowing White to double rooks on the c-file. (Levenfish – Lisitsin, Moscow 1948)

(107)** Trapped piece, fork

The Black knight has nowhere to go. **1.h5! e4 2.hxg6 hxg6** [2...exd3? 3.g7 forks the Black rooks] **3.Rxh8 Rxh8 4.Bf1.** White is a piece ahead.

(108)**** Liberating pawn offer

1...e6! frees the c7 knight, challenges the White pawn front, and opens the d8–h4 diagonal for the Black queen. White must not accept the offered a-pawn, as **2.dxe6 Nxe6 3.Rxa6 Bxe4 4.fxe4 Qh4 5.Nf3 Nxf3+ 6.Bxf3 Be5** gives Black a winning attack.

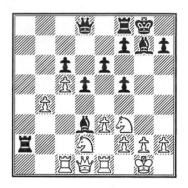

109. White to move

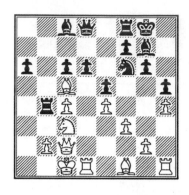

112. Black to move

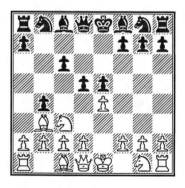

110. White to move

113. White to move

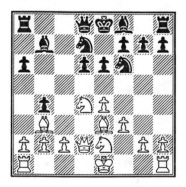

111. Black to move

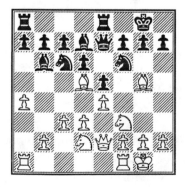

114. Black to move

(109)* Double attack
1.Qb3 attacks the loose bishop and rook. White is up by the exchange following **1...Rxd2 2.Nxd2**.

(110)** Trapped piece
1.Nxd5!. White wins at least a pawn, for example **1...cxd5 2.Bxd5** (attacking the a8 rook) **Bg4!? 3.Qxg4 Nf6 4.Qh4 Nxd5 5.Qxd8+ Kxd8 6.exd5**.

(111)** Thematic central advance
In the open Sicilian, a typical freeing move for Black is ...d6-d5, and Black should constantly check whether it can be favorably achieved. In the present case, Black is at least equal after **1...d5! 2.exd5 Nxd5 3.0–0–0 Nc5**. He possesses the sole remaining center pawn, his pieces have decent squares, and he will soon enjoy the bishop pair advantage.

(112)** Material sac for piece activity
Rather than retreat the attacked rook, Black should prefer **1...dxc5! 2.Rxd8 Rxd8 3.Bd3 Bh6+ 4.Kb1 Be6**. For the modest material investment, Black has a pair of slashing bishops and two beautiful files for his rooks. His knight may come around to d6, hitting the target on c4. His doubled pawns are hardly a weakness here. On the other hand, White's bishop is hemmed in by his own pawns, his knight has little scope, and his queen is relegated to passive defense.

(113)* Restrict enemy piece
After **1.a4!** the Black knight has no safe moves. White will proceed to harass the knight and Black's weak pawns, while his own knight has a fine post at c4.

(114)** A stitch in time
1...a6 [or 1...a5]. Black must move his a-pawn, to prevent 1.Bxc6 Bxc6 2.a5 Bc5 3.b4 trapping the bishop.

115. Black to move

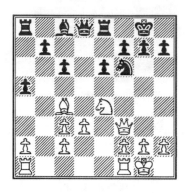

118. Black to move

116. Black to move

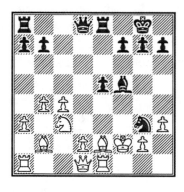

119. Black to move

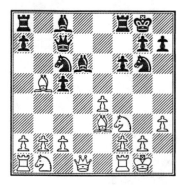

117. White to move

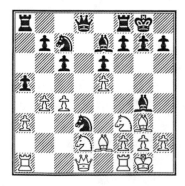

120. White to move

(115)** Don't push *this* passed pawn!
The Black king will dash over to the kingside to capture the
White pawn and escort his own h-pawn to the first rank.
Meanwhile, the White monarch wants to capture the b-pawn, and
then hurry to the corner to intercept advancing h-pawn. It's a
simple foot race, one that Black happens to win as follows:
**1...Kd5 2.Kb4 Ke4 3.Kb5 Kf4 4.Kxb6 Kg4 5.Kc5 Kxh4 6.Kd4
Kg3 7.Ke3 h4 8.Ke2 h3 9.Kf1 h2** and the pawn promotes.
Pushing the b-pawn first, however, actually throws away the
win, as then the White king needs fewer steps to get back to the
corner: 1...b5?? 2.Kb3 Kd4 3.Kb4 Ke4 4.Kxb5 Kf4 5.Kc4 Kg4
6.Kd3 Kxh4 7.Ke2 Kg3 8.Kf1 h4 [or 8...Kh2 9.Kf2 draw] 9.Kg1
and White alternates between g1 and h1 (or is stalemated) for the
draw.

(116)**** *Zugzwang*, passed pawn
Black wins by **1...c4!** (creating a passed pawn, and freeing c5 for
his king) [1...Kc7? 2.Kb5 (not 2.Kxa5? c4!) 2...Kb7 3.a4 is only
a draw] **2.dxc4** [2.Kxa5 c3] **2...Kc7! 3.Kb3** [3.c5 dxc5 4.Kb3
Kd6 5.Kc4 a4 puts White in *zugzwang*, and he must surrender
the d-pawn] **3...Kb6! 4.a4** [or 4.Kc2 Kc5 5.Kb3 a4+ 6.Kxa4
Kxc4] **4...Kc5** *zugzwang!* **5.Kc2 Kxc4.**

(117)* Double attack
1.Qd5+ picks up the knight on c6.

(118)** The trap fails
Black must reject 1...b5? intending to trap the bishop by 2.Bb3??
2...a4. Instead White has **2.Bxb5!**, as 2...cxb5? 3.Nxf6+ Qxf6
4.Qxa8 wins the exchange and a pawn. A better try for Black
would be **1...Nd5 2.d4 e5**, freeing his bishop and fighting for a
share of the center.

(119)** Dovetail mate
1...Qd4+ 2.Kxg3 Qf4 mate.

(120)** Trapped piece
1.Ne4! Nb2 2.Qb3 traps the Black knight.

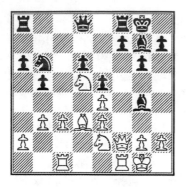

121. Black to move

124. Black to move

122. White to move

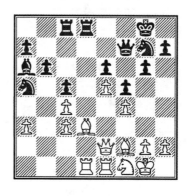

125. Black to move

123. Black to move

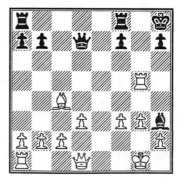

126. Black to move

(121)*** Exploit weaknesses

Black can exploit the weakness of e3, d5 and f2 by **1...f5!**. White cannot avoid material loss: **2.Qe1** [2.Nxb6 Qxb6 3.exf5 Bh6 4.Kh1 Bxe3 winning the exchange; 2.Qg3 Nxd5 3.exd5 e4 winning a piece (as the bishop guards the knight on c2)] **2...Nxd5 3.exd5 Qb6 4.Ng3 Bh6** and the e3 pawn falls with more losses to follow.

(122)**** The Greek Gift

1.Bxh7+! Kxh7 [1...Kh8 2.Qh4 Nef5 3.Qh5 Nh6 4.Bxh6 gxh6 5.Qxh6 Re8 6.Bf5+ Kg8 7.Ng5 winning] **2.Qh4+ Kg8** [2...Kg6 3.Ne5+ Kf5 4.Qf4 mate] **3.Ng5 Re8 4.Qh7+ Kf8 5.Qh8+ Ng8 6.Nh7+ Ke7 7.Bg5+ f6** [7...Nf6 8.Bxf6+ gxf6 9.Qxf6 mate] **8.Qxg7+ Nf7 9.Bxf6+ Kd6 10.Bxd8** winning.

(123)** King in the open

1...Ng5+ [1...Rf8+? would allow White to escape by 2.Kg2] **2.Kg2** [2.Kf4 Re4+ 3.Kxg5 Qf5 mate; 2.Kg3 Qxh3+ 3.Kf4 Qh4 mate] **2...Qxh3+ 3.Kg1 Nf3** mate.

(124)*** Fork, skewer, discovered attack

1...e5! 2.Bxe5 [2.Bg3 e4 forks two pieces; 2.Nxe5 Nh5 Black will pick off one of the enemy knights] **2...Nxe5 3.Nxe5 Ng4** (unleashing the powerful g7 bishop) **4.f4** [4.Nxg4 allows Bxc3+ 5.Kf1 Bxg4 6.Qxg4 Bxa1 and wins] **4...Nxe5 5.fxe5 Bxe5 6.Qd2 d4! 7.exd4** [7.Ne2 dxe3 8.Qxe3 Bxa1 winning] **7...Qxd4** winning a piece.

(125)**** Meet positional threat

White threatens Bh4! hitting some sensitive dark squares and preventing Black from doubling rooks on the d-file. Black's solution is **1...Nh5!!** tying the White bishop to passive defense of the f4 pawn (2.g2-g3 is even worse). There followed **2.Bg3 Qe8 3.Ne3 Qa4** and Black eventually won. (Botvinnik – Reshevsky, Moscow 1948)

(126)** Exposed king

1...Qd4+ 2.Kh1 Qf2 3.Qg1 Qxf3+ 4.Qg2 Qxg2 mate.

127. White to move

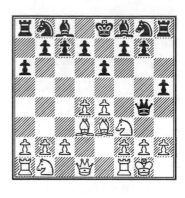

130. White to move

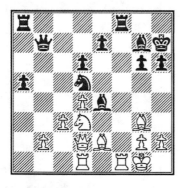

128. Black to move

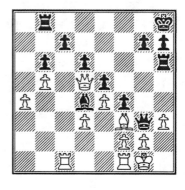

131. White to move

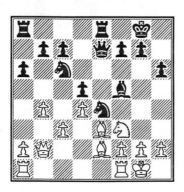

129. Black to move

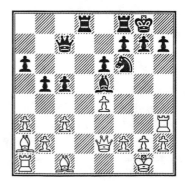

132. Black to move

(127)*** Promotion, win back a pawn

White cannot prevent the loss of his d6 pawn. However, he can maintain the material balance by **1.Re1! f6 2.f4 Rd8** [the tactical point being 2...exf4?? 3.d7 Rd8 4.Re8+ and wins] **3.fxe5 fxe5 4.Rxe5 Rxd6 5.Re7**.

(128)*** Double check, mate

Black wins a pawn with **1...Bxg2!**, since **2.Kxg2?** is punished by **2...Ne3+ 3.Kh3 Qd7+** with mate to follow.

(129)** Remove the guard, discovered attack

1...Nxf2! picks up a pawn. If the knight is taken (in any of the three ways), then Black will capture one of the bishops.

(130)** Trapped piece

White surely has a huge advantage after any routine developing move. Better still, he can trap the enemy queen as follows: **1.h3! Qg6 2.e5 f5 3.exf6 Qxf6** [or 3...Qf7 4.Ne5] **4.Bg5 Qf7 5.Ne5**.

(131)*** Repel enemy attack

Black threatens ...Rxh3 with devastating consequences. The best defense is **1.Qxd4!** to relieve the agonizing pin on f2. Now the Black queen is under attack [after 1.Rc2? Rxh3 Black's assault rages on, and this defensive idea is no longer available]. **1...Qxf3** (otherwise Black is just a piece down) **2.gxf3 exd4 3.Rxc7!**. White should win the resulting endgame.

(132)** Don't grab the pawn!

1...Nxe4?? may appear to win a pawn due to 2.Qxe4?? Rd1 mate. But instead of falling for the back rank mate, White can play 2.f4! getting a piece for two pawns. Better tries for Black are **1...Bf4** to prevent Bc1-g5xf6, and **1...c4** to shut the a2 bishop out of play.

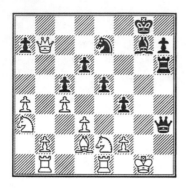

133. Black to move

136. White to move

134. White to move

137. Black to move

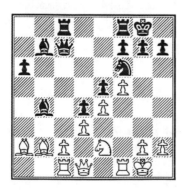

135. Black to move

138. White to move

(133)*** Interference
Black quickest win is **1...d5!** interfering with the White queen's defense against mate [1...f3 2.Qxf3 Qxf3 3.Bxh6 Bxh6 also wins] **2.Qa8+ Kf7 3.Ng3 f3 4.Qxd5+ Nxd5** mate next move.

(134)*** Control crucial square
The only way to make progress is **1.Kg6!!** paradoxically moving away from the pawns. Black must concede the g5 square, and then lose the g-pawn. One White pawn will survive to ensure the win. **1...Kf3** [1...Ke4 2.Kg5 Kf3 3.Kf5 Kg2 4.Kxg4] **2.Kg5 Kxf2 3.Kxg4** with victory in sight.

(135)** Fork, trapped piece
1...Ng4! wins the exchange: **2.Rf3** (since ...Ne3 was threatened) **2...Ne3 3.Rxe3** (forced, as White's queen is trapped) **3...dxe3**.

(136)** Disarm enemy combination
Black is threatening 1...Rxf3! winning a piece, since 2.gxf3? drops the queen to 2...Qg6+ 3.Kh1 Ng3+. White can prevent material loss by, for example, **1.Nd2** (moving the knight away), **1.Qd1** (removing the queen from the potential discovered attack), or **1.Rac1** (protecting the queen).

(137)*** Prevent counterplay
1...g5!! kills counterplay by preventing White from building the advanced pawn chain d6-e5-f4. The continuation might be **2.g3 g4! 3.h3 h5!**.

(138)**** Hanging pawns advance
White's hanging pawns could become a weakness. But on the other hand, they control a quartet of important squares, and their potential to advance is a constant menace to Black. A case in point: **1.d5! Nc5** [1...exd5 2.Nd4 Nhf6 3.Nf5 Qf8 4.Ne7+ picking up the exchange] **2.Ng5 g6 3.Be2 Ng7 4.Qd4**. The queen takes up the newly vacated d4 square. White has an impressive attack. The finish was **4...Qf8 5.Qh4 h5 6.Bg4!! f5 7.Nxe6 Ngxe6 8.dxc6 Rc8 9.Bxh5 Qh6 10.Qf6 f4 11.Qf7** mate. (Gligorić – Keres, Zagreb 1948)

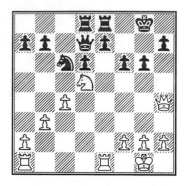

139. White to move

142. Black to move

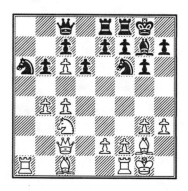

140. White to move

143. White to move

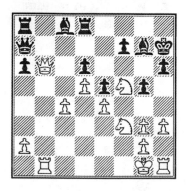

141. Black to move

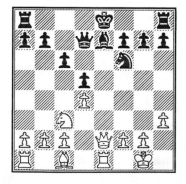

144. Black to move

(139)** Fork, remove the guard

But for the e7 pawn, Nxf6+ would fork the Black king and queen. Hence **1.Rxe7! Rxe7 2.Nxf6+.**

(140)** Imprison enemy piece

1.Ra4! (defending b4 and preparing to drive back the knight by Qa2) [1.Qa4! Nb8 2.b5 achieves the same thing] **1...Nb8 2.b5.** Now the knight is completely locked out of play. (Alekhine – Schwartz, London 1926)

(141)** Double attack

1...Qxb6+ 2.Rxb6 Bxf5 3.exf5 e4 wins material, as Black now threatens both ...Bd4+ and ...exf3.

(142)*** Exposed king

1...Qe3! wins heavy material, due to the threat of ...Rf8+: **2.g3** [2.Qe2 Rf8+ 3.Ke1 Qc3+ 4.Kd1 Qxa1+ and Black is up a rook; 2.Qf3 Rf8 wins the queen] **2...Rf8+ 3.Kg2 Rf2+ 4.Kh1** [4.Kg1 Re2+ 5.Kh1 Qf3+ 6.Kg1 Qg2 mate] **4...Qe4+** mating.

(143)*** Foil enemy plan

Black threatens to play ...e5-e4, followed by ...Bf5 (skewering the White queen and rook), and eventually ...exd4, opening the long diagonal for his dark-squared bishop. **1.Bh3!** stops this plan by pinning the e-pawn to the defender of b7. (Tal – Botvinnik, Moscow 1960)

(144)** Break the pin

The pin along the e-file is obviously a worry for Black. Now is his last chance to skip away by **1...0–0!** with at least an equal position [but on other moves White plays 2.Bg5 or 2.Bf4, and then the Black king really is stuck in the middle]. The bishop cannot be captured, as **2.Qxe7?? Rfe8** wins material for Black.

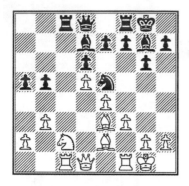

145. White to move

148. Black to move

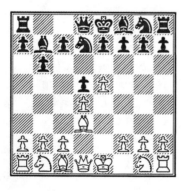

146. White to move

149. White to move

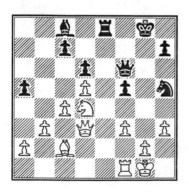

147. Black to move

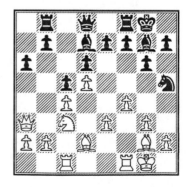

150. Black to move

(145)** Trapped piece
1.f4! traps the knight on e5. Note that after **1...Ng4!? 2.Bxg4 Bxg4 3.Qxg4 Bb2 4.f5 Bxc1 5.Rxc1** White has captured two minor pieces for a rook.

(146)** Weaken enemy position
White causes maximum misery by **1.e6!** Ndf6 [not 1...fxe6?? 2.Qh5+ g6 3.Qxg6+ hxg6 4.Bxg6 mate] **2.exf7+ Kxf7 3.Nf3**. Black's king is exposed, and White will hammer the weak squares e5 and e6.

(147)** Fork
1...Nf4! 2.Qd2 Qxd4+! 3.Qxd4 Ne2+ nets a piece.

(148)* Pin, remove the guard
1...c5 hits a defender of the pinned e4 knight, winning material: **2.Rxd6 Rxd6 3.f3 Rxd1+ 4.Bxd1 Bxe4 5.fxe4.**

(149)**** Scrape out a draw
White's advanced pawns are doomed. However, White can ensure a draw by **1.Rf4+!!** [1.Rh4 Rxc6 2.Rxh7+ Ke6 3.h4 Rd6 4.h5 gxh5 5.Rxh5 should also be a draw, but Black can prolong the agony] **1...Ke7** [1...Kg7 2.Re4 Rxc6 3.Re8 Nf7 4.d8Q Nxd8 5.Rxd8 is a draw] **2.Re4+** (the point: White's rook goes to e4 with check, and hence it reaches e8 in time to attack the knight) **2...Kd6 3.Re8 Nxc6 4.d8Q+ Nxd8 5.Rxd8+**, with a book draw.

(150)*** Good time for a break
Black should play the desired break **1...b5!** even though the a6 pawn is left undefended: **2.Qxa6?** would be punished by **2...b4 3.Nb5 Ra8 4.Qb7 Rxa2 5.Rb1 Bxb2.**

151. White to move

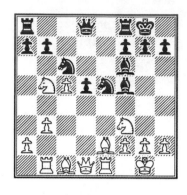

154. White to move

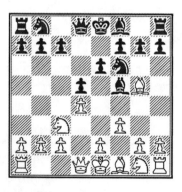

152. White to move

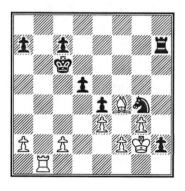

155. Black to move

153. White to move

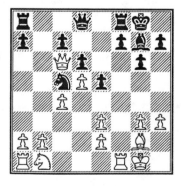

156. Black to move

(151)* Double attack
1.Nxe7 Kxe7 2.Bc5+ wins a piece.

(152)** Pin, double attack
1.e4! wins a piece, for if 1...Bg6 [or 1...dxc4 2.fxc4 Bg4 3.Bxf6] then 2.e5.

(153)** Outflanking
The White king must reach d6, e6 or f6 (or, in principle, a6 or b6) in order to "outflank" his counterpart. 1.Kf5! [however, after 1.Ke5? Ke7 White can make no progress] 1...Ke7 2.Ke5 Kd7 3.Kf6 Kd8 4.Ke6 Kc7 5.Ke7 Kc8 6.Kd6 Kb7 7.Kd7 and Black is forced to relinquish his pawns.

(154)**** Make lemonade
White cannot avoid losing the exchange. However, 1.Rb2!! minimizes the damage by getting Black's better bishop for the rook. After 1...Nxf3+ 2.Bxf3 Bxb2 3.Bxb2 Be6 4.Nd6 all of White's pieces are wonderfully positioned.

(155)* Overworked piece
The White king cannot cover both f2 and the promotion square. 1...Nxf2! 2.Kxf2 h1Q 3.Rxh1 Rxh1 with a straightforward win.

(156)** Trapped piece
The White queen is stuck at c6. Nothing can prevent her demise after 1...Rb8! followed by ...Rb6.

157. White to move

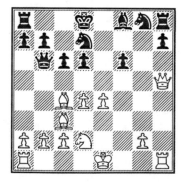

160. White to move

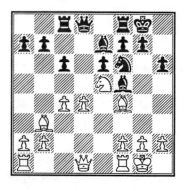

158. Black to move

161. White to move

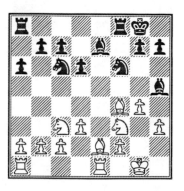

159. Black to move

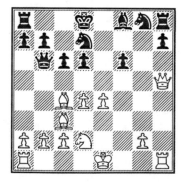

162. White to move

(157)*** Defensive sac
White's best hope to fight for a draw is **1.Rxc3!** [1.Kb2 would allow 1...c4 2.Rd2 e3 and Black crashes through] **1...dxc3 2.Qxc3**. White has survival chances due to his advanced queenside pawns.

(158)** Thematic pawn advance
This pawn structure can arise from a wide variety of openings, including the French, Alekhine, Caro-Kann and Scandinavian defenses. Black's usual objective going into the middlegame is to achieve the ...c6-c5 thrust (or less commonly,...e6-e5). In the present case, **1...c5!** gives Black a comfortable game. **2.dxc5** [after 2.d5 exd5 3.cxd5 Bd6 White has to be mindful of the push ...c5-c4, and of the rickety material on d5, e5 and f4] **2...Bxc5** and Black has two active bishops and play against the c4 pawn. (Gligorić – Smyslov, Moscow 1963)

(159)*** Don't eat poisoned pawns
Black should not snatch pawns by 1...Nxg4? 2.hxg4 Bxg4, intending to recapture a piece on the f-file. White can actually keep the extra piece: 3.Bg5! Bxf3 [3...Bxg5 4.Nxg5] 4.Bxe7 Nxe7 5.Bxf3 Rxf3 6.Rxe7. The simple retreat **1...Bf7** is better.

(160)*** The principle of two weaknesses
White's threat of Ne3-f5xh6 tethers the Black knight to g7, and forces the Black king to stay near the f-file. To win, White opens a second front by **1.Ke2!**, heading for c3 to support the b3-b4 break. (Kasparov – Hübner, Hamburg 1985)

(161)* Fork
White wins a piece by **1.d4**, for example, **1...exd4 2.exd4 Bb6 3.d5**.

(162)* Pin
1.Ba5 is the most forceful option, winning the queen.

66

163. Black to move

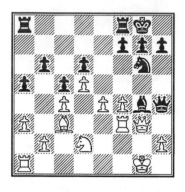

166. White to move

164. White to move

167. Black to move

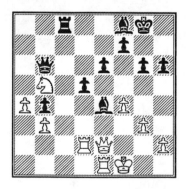

165. Black to move

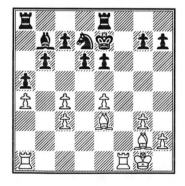

168. White to move

(163)*** Promote the right pawn
Both sides will promote after 1...Kc3? 2.Kxh5; or 1...b5?! 2.a5!.
The best approach is **1...a5! 2.Kxh5 b5 3.axb5** [3.Kxg4 bxa4 is
similar] **3...Kxb5 4.Kxg4 a4**. The incipient Black queen will
cover White's promotion square h8 for an easy win.

(164)*** Deflection, remove the guard
The rook at f7 strains to defend both d7 and f4. White wins
material by **1.Rxd7! Rxd7 2.Rxd3 cxd3 3.Kxf4**. White will now
shore up his queenside and press his material advantage.

(165)**** Offer another exchange
Black has already sacrificed an exchange for a passed pawn and
the bishop pair. But because of White's well placed knight it is
difficult for Black to make progress. Black therefore offers a
second exchange: **1...Rc3!! 2.Nxc3** [refusing the offered material
doesn't help: 2.Nd4 Bc5 3.Red1 Bxd4 4.Rxd4 Rxb3] **2...bxc3**
and the mighty bishops will escort a pawn through. (Trojanescu
– Petrosian, Bucharest 1953)

(166)** Mate, pin
1.Qxh4 Nxh4 2.Rg3 f5 [2...Bd7 allows 3.Rxg7+ Kh8 4.Rxf7+
Kg8 5.Rg7+ Kh8 6.Rg5+ Rf6 7.Bxf6 mate] **3.h3** winning a
piece.

(167)** Pin, fork, discovered attack
1...e5! 2.Bg5 [2.Bh2?? allows the fork 2...e4; 2.dxe5?? loses to
2...dxc5 with an attack on each bishop] **2...exd4** and White is a
pawn down.

(168)** Discovered attack, pin
1.Bg5+ Nf6 2.e5 wins a piece.

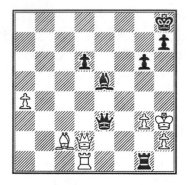

169. Black to move

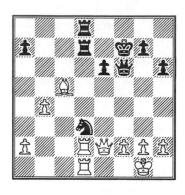

172. Black to move

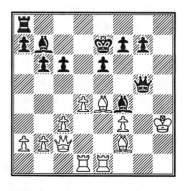

170. White to move

173. Black to move

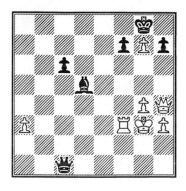

171. Black to move

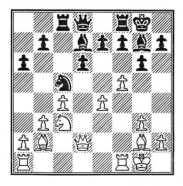

174. White to move

(169)* Final rook offer
1...Rxg3+! 2.Kh4 [2.hxg3 Qxg3 mate] **2...Bf6** mate.

(170)** Interference, pin
1.Bh4! Rh8 2.Bh7! wins the Black queen.

(171)** Skewer, double attack
Rather than merely exchange bishop for rook, Black can win the
rook outright by **1...Qe1+! 2.Rf2 Qe5+ 3.Rf4 Qe3+ 4.Kh2
Qxf4+**.

(172)** Weak back rank, overworked piece
White is a piece down after **1...Nxc5**, for if **2.bxc5? Rxd2
3.Rxd2 Rxd2**, then White cannot both recapture the rook and
defend the vulnerable first rank.

(173)**** Do not hurry
Rather than capture immediately at d4, Black first ties down the
White rook, and improves his king position. **1...Rh3!** [on
1...Kxd4? 2.Rg4+ Kd5 3.Rh4 White gets an outside passed
pawn, probably enough to secure a draw] **2.Rd2 Kc4 3.Kc1
Rh4**. Black next captures the d-pawn under much better
circumstances. (Smyslov – Keres, Moscow/Leningrad 1941)

(174)*** Create outpost
1.f6! forces the removal of Black's e-pawn, leaving White in sole
possession of the excellent d5 outpost. **1...exf6** [much worse is
1...Bxf6 2.Rxf6! exf6 3.Nd5 when mate at g7 is looming; Black
is similarly doomed after 1...Bh8 2.fxe7 Qxe7 3.Nd5 Qe6
4.Nf6+] **2.Nd5** and White won shortly. (Smyslov – Timman,
Moscow 1981)

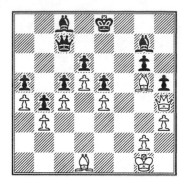

175. White to move

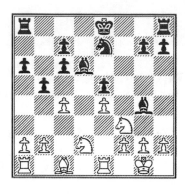

178. White to move

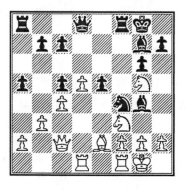

176. Black to move

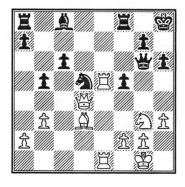

179. Black to move

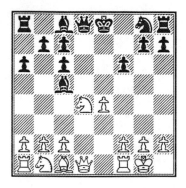

177. White to move

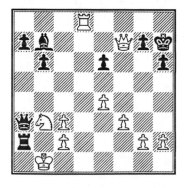

180. White to move

(175)** Exchange bad bishop for good
1.g4! forces the exchange of White's bad bishop for Black's good bishop. The sequel was **1...hxg4 2.Bxg4 Bxg4 3.Qxg4 Qd7 4.Qxd7+ Kxd7**. With the superior minor piece by far, White won in a further 10 moves. (Suetin – Matanović, Belgrade 1974)

(176)* Pin
1...Nxe2+ 2.Qxe2 Qxg5 puts Black a piece up.

(177)* Double attack
The opening moves were 1.e4 e5 2.Nf3 Nc6 3.Bb5 a6 4.Bxc6 dxc6 5.0–0 f6 6.d4 exd4 7.Nxd4 Bc5?? (D). White continued **8.Qh5+** winning the bishop.

(178)** Passed pawn, outpost, open file
White does well to play **1.c5! Bxc5 2.Nxe5** obtaining a protected passed pawn, a nice square for his knight, and a semi-open file toward Black's doubled backward pawns.

(179)* A little housekeeping
1...a6 [or 1...b4] is a necessary step, as the c6 pawn is overworked, defending both b5 and d5.

(180)** By a razor's edge
White lands the first punch by **1.Qg8+ Kg6 2.Qxe6+ Kh7** [2...Kg5 3.Qf5+ Kh4 4.Qg4 mate] **3.Qf5+ g6 4.Qf7** mate.

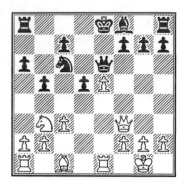

181. White to move

184. Black to move

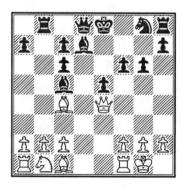

182. White to move

185. Black to move

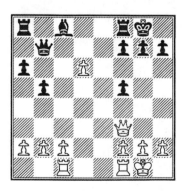

183. White to move

186. White to move

(181)*** Disrupt enemy plans

Black's counterplay will be based, in part, on a queenside expansion. **1.Be3!** takes control of the important square c5. There followed **1...Be7** [the e5 pawn is taboo: 1...Qxe5?? drops the queen to 2.Bd4; while 1...Nxe5? loses to 2.Qg3! when the knight will be pinned along the e-file and captured] **2.Nc5 Bxc5 3.Bxc5.** Black has difficulty castling short and arranging the ...c7-c5 advance.

(182)* Double attack

White wins a piece as follows: **1.Bxg8! Rxg8 2.Qc4.**

(183)** Promotion, pin, remove the guard

Momentarily down a piece, White's best chance is **1.d7!** Qxf3 [or 1...Bxd7?? 2.Qxb7; 1...Qxd7?? 2.Qxa8] **2.dxc8Q Qxg2+ 3.Kxg2 Raxc8.**

(184)*** Exposed king

1...Qf3! [White is still dangerous after the queen swap 1...Nxe1? 2.gxf4 Rxf4 3.Rxg6 Kh7 4.Rc6] **2.Qa1 Qe3+ 3.Kg2** [3.Kh1 Nf2+ 4.Kg2 Qe4+ 5.Kf1 Nh3+ mating next move] **3...Rf2+ 4.Kh3** [4.Kh1 Qf3+ 5.Kg1 Qg2 mate] **4...Nf4+ 5.Kg4 Qe2+ 6.Kh4 Rxh2** mate.

(185)* Rook behind passed pawn

Rooks generally belong behind passed pawns, including those of the enemy. **1...Rc1+ 2.Kh2 Ra1** gives Black the best chance to split the point.

(186)** Change key squares

1.c6! [1.Ke3? Kd5 2.Kd3 Kxc5 3.Kc3 d6 and Black wins, as his king has reached one of the "key squares" c5, d5 and e5 of his pawn] **1...dxc6 2.Ke3** earns a draw. The Black king has been prevented from reaching the new key squares b4, c4 and d4.

187. White to move

190. White to move

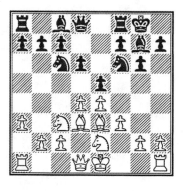

188. Black to move

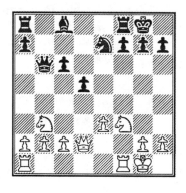

191. White to move

189. White to move

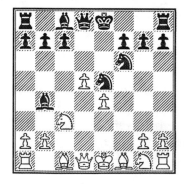

192. White to move

(187)** Corridor mate
1.Rf6+ Kh5 2.Ng7+ Kh4 3.Rh6 mate.

(188)** Strike at enemy pawn center
1...d5! [or exchanging on d4 first] will either liquidate White's two-pawn center, or leave White with an isolated e-pawn after ...dxe4 and fxe4, thus ensuring equality. Opening the center also reduces White's prospects of attacking on the kingside.

(189)* Discovered check, mate
1.Bh7+ Kh8 2.Bg6+ Kg8 3.Qh7 mate.

(190)*** Better IQP middlegame
After the forced series of exchanges **1.cxd5 cxd5** [1...Nxd5? loses material: 2.Nc4 Bc7 3.e4 N5f6 4.Nfxe5 Nxe5 5.dxe5; 1...e4? 2.dxc6 loses a pawn] **2.dxe5 Nxe5 3.Nxe5 Bxe5 4.Bxe5 Rxe5 5.Nf3** White has the favorable side of an isolated queen pawn middlegame. The piece exchanges have served to dilute Black's dynamic potential. White furthermore has the fine d4 square for his knight, and he possesses the better bishop.

(191)*** Fix favorable pawn structure
1.Qc3! fixes in place the Black c- and d-pawns, which get in the way of Black's minor pieces. White's knights will occupy the lovely outposts at c5 and d4. (Botvinnik – Boleslavsky, Moscow 1941).

(192)* Double attack
1.Qa4+ wins a piece.

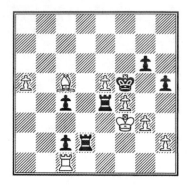

193. Black to move

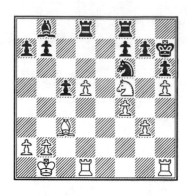

196. White to move

194. Black to move

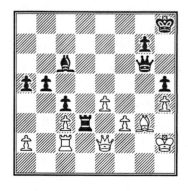

197. Black to move

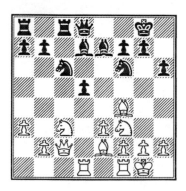

195. White to move

198. Black to move

(193)** Deflection, promotion

The simplest win is **1...Re1!** (deflecting the White rook from the promotion square) **2.Rxe1 Rd1!**.

(194)* Queen sac, promotion

1...Qb1+ 2.Rxb1 axb1Q mate.

(195)*** Facing an IQP, trade minor pieces

A player facing an enemy isolated queen pawn should generally seek to exchange minor pieces, thereby reducing his opponent's attacking prospects, and bringing the position closer to an endgame, where the weakness of the isolated pawn is more acutely felt. White achieved this here by **1.Ne5! Be6 2.Nxc6 Rxc6** [the tactical point is that recapturing with a pawn drops the exchange: 2...bxc6?? 3.Ba6]. (Karpov – Spassky, Montréal 1979)

(196)** Superior piece activity

After **1.Bxf6! gxf6 2.d6 Rd7 3.Rhe1** White has a dangerous passed pawn; he controls the open file; and his knight is unassailable on its fine outpost. By contrast Black's king is stuck to h6; his rooks are relegated to defensive duties; and his bishop is rather hemmed in.

(197)*** The tactic fails, shield king

The tactical shot 1...Rxf3?? 2.Qxf3 Bxe4 fails due to 3.Qf8+. This suggests **1...Kh7!**, tucking the king away so that such tactical ideas are enabled.

(198)** Undefended pawn

Black can safely grab a pawn by **1...Nb4! 2.Qe2** [2.Nxe4?? drops the exchange to 2...Nxd3 3.Nxd6 Nxc1; 2.Qb1?? hangs the d2 knight] **2...Rxc1** [Black is a piece down after 2...Nxa2?? 3.Rxc7 Qxc7 4.Nxe4] **3.Rxc1 Nxa2**.

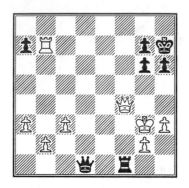

199. White to move

202. Black to move

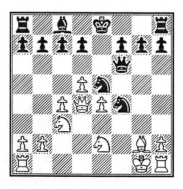

200. Black to move

203. Black to move

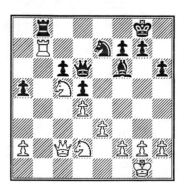

201. White to move

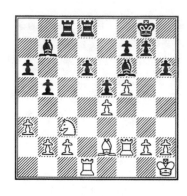

204. White to move

(199)*** Force winning endgame
White's queenside pawn majority is a long term asset, but in the meantime he must beware of perpetual check and mating threats due to his exposed king. The only way to win is **1.Qe5!**. White threatens mate at g7. This forces **1...Qe1+** and simplification to an easily won endgame [1...Rf6?? 2.Qxf6; 1...Qd3+? 2.Kh2] **2.Qxe1 Rxe1 3.Rxa7**.

(200)** Deflection, fork
1...Nh3+! 2.Bxh3 Nf3+ 3.Kg2 Nxd4.

(201)* Trapped piece
1.Rd7! traps the Black queen.

(202)*** Sac creates targets, activity
At the board Black chose the pawn sac **1...d5!** with the idea **2.exd5** [the game continued 2.Nxd5 Bxd5 3.exd5 Rxc2 4.b3 e4 and Black won] **2...e4**, opening up the position for his bishop pair, and underscoring the weakness of White's pawns. Also good is the typical exchange sac 1...Rxc3!? 2.bxc3 Bxe4. (Petrosian – Smyslov, Moscow 1949)

(203)** The Philidor Position
The surest way to draw is **1...Rb6!** preventing the White king from reaching the 6th rank. (Black can also draw after 1...Rb1, but only with very precise play.) After **2.e6** (what else can White try?), Black responds **2...Rb1!**. Now the White king has no cover from the rook's checks.

(204)*** The Lucena Position
This is generally the finish to aim for when you're a pawn up in a rook endgame. **1.Rc2+!** first cuts off the Black king. **1...Kb7** [1...Kd6 loses immediately due to 2.Kd8] **2.Rc4!** The rook is placed on the 4th rank, out of the Black king's reach, to shield his own king from checks at the crucial moment. **2...Rf2 3.Kd7 Rd2+ 4.Ke6 Re2+ 5.Kd6 Rd2+ 6.Ke5 Re2+ 7.Re4** and the pawn will promote.

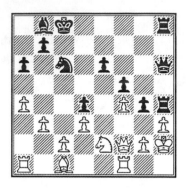

205. Black to move

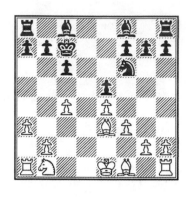

208. Black to move

206. White to move

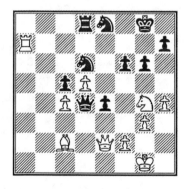

209. White to move

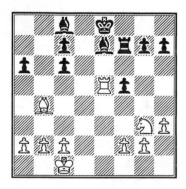

207. White to move

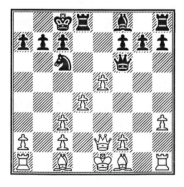

210. Black to move

(205)* Rook sac
1...Rxh3+! 2.gxh3 Qxh3+ 3.Kg1 Qh1 mate.

(206)** Prevent counterplay
1.Bc3! prevents ...Rd2 and the unfavorable complications that would follow. (Kasparov – Vukić, Skara Echt 1980)

(207)** Overworked piece
Black's rook is overworked, guarding both e7 and f5. White nets a pawn by **1.Nxf5!** [1.Nh5! also wins a pawn after two exchanges at e7], for example **1...Bxf5 2.Bxe7 Rxe7 3.Rxf5**.

(208)**** Obtain superior minor pieces
1...Nd7!!. This move inhibits the c4-c5 advance, thereby restricting White's light-squared bishop; it also prepares ...Bc5, to eliminate White's "good" bishop. The game continued **2.Nd2 a5!** (to prevent b2-b4) **3.Be2 a4! 4.Kf2 Bc5! 5.Bxc5 Nxc5**. Black has superior minor pieces. The pawn on a4 ensures that the powerfully posted knight cannot be chased away. (Domenech – Flohr, Rosas 1935)

(209)*** Fork, overworked piece
The knight on d6 cannot adequately defend both e4 and f7. **1.Nh6+** [or 1.Bxe4! first] **1...Kh8 2.Bxe4** and White has won a pawn, as after **2...Nxe4??** [2...Qxe4?? 3.Qxe4 Nxe4 4.Nf7+ Kg8 5.Nxd8 is similar] **3.Nf7+ Kg8 4.Nxd8** White wins the exchange as well.

(210)*** Double attacks
White has built up a formidable pawn front, and is threatening the Black queen. Retreating the queen would only cement White's overwhelming presence the center. Instead, Black can leverage the looseness of White's rooks by **1...Nxe5!**. The knight should not be taken. After **2.Bg2** [2.Qxe5? Qf3 wins a rook by hitting h1 and c3; or 2.dxe5 Qc6 also winning a rook] **2...Nd7 3.0–0 c6** Black is still in the game.

211. Black to move

214. Black to move

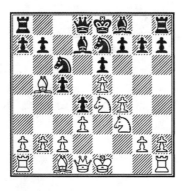

212. Black to move

215. White to move

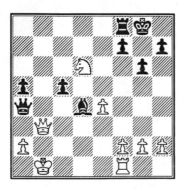

213. Black to move

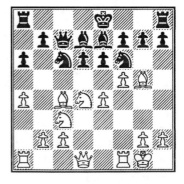

216. Black to move

(211)* Double attack
The double attack **1...Rd3** wins a pawn.

(212)** Blunder check
Black had better do something about White's threat of Nd6 mate.
1...Qa5+?? would be a terrible mistake, as White has **2.Bd2 Qb6**
[2...Qxb5?? drops the queen to 3.Nd6+] **3.Nd6+ Kd8 4.Nxf7+**
still winning material. Better is **1...Nd5** to defend d6.

(213)*** Loose material, exposed king
White's knight and rook are unprotected, his king is exposed, and
he has loose pawns; Black's king is secure, his bishop is well
posted, and his rook has prospects on the open b-file. From
Black's point of view, trading queens would dissipate these
assets; instead, he should look for a way into convert them to
hard currency. **1...Qc6!** is one way to do it [1...Qd7 is also good].
2.Nc4 [or 2.Qd5 Qb6+ 3.Kc2 Qb2+ 4.Kd1 Qb1+ 5.Ke2 Qc2+
6.Kf3 Qd3+ picking up the rook] **2...Qxe4+ 3.Kc1 Qxg2 4.Qd3
Qxh2**. Black is up three pawns and has lasting pressure.

(214)** Pin, deflection
1...Re2+ 2.Kg3 h4+! (deflection) [2...Qe5+ also wins] **3.Kxh4**
[3.Kf4 Qe5 mate] **3...Qxf3**.

(215)** Promotion, weak back rank
Black's vulnerable back rank allows **1.Qxg8! Rxg8 2.Rf8+ Rxf8**
[2...Bd8 3.Rxg8 a6 4.Rxd8+ Ka7 5.e8Q] **3.exf8Q+ Bd8**. From
here the simplest win would be **4.Qf4+ Bc7 5.Qxc7+ Qxc7
6.Rxc7 Kxc7 7.gxh4**.

(216)** Create two threats
1...Nxd4 2.Qxd4 d5 wins material, as Black threatens both
...dxc4 and ...Bc5.

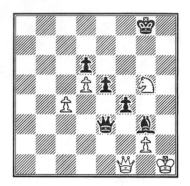

217. Black to move

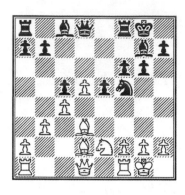

220. White to move

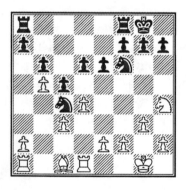

218. Black to move

221. White to move

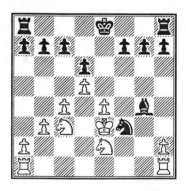

219. White to move

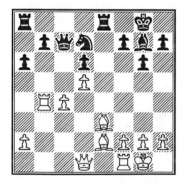

222. Black to move

(217)*** Discovered attack, mate, remove the guard
1...f3! packs the triple threat of ...Qxg5, ...f3-f2, and (indirectly) ...Qh6+. Now **2.Nxf3** [2.Nh3 f2 and Black must give up the knight to stop Qe1] **2...Qh6+ 3.Kg1 e4** wins the knight, which is held to the defense of h2.

(218)** Open file toward targets
1...a6! 2.bxa6 Rxa6. Black has opened the a-file to go after the weak pawns at a2 and c3. The finish was **3.dxc5 bxc5 4.Ng2 Nd5 5.Rd3 Rfa8 6.e4 Ne5!** winning material. (Mattison – Alekhine, Carlsbad 1929)

(219)* Remove the guard
1.h3 Bh5 2.Ng3. White will win a piece.

(220)*** Eliminate potential blockader
One of White's chief strategic assets is his passed pawn on d5. Knights are generally the best blockaders of passed pawns, and indeed the knight on f5 is poised to assume this role on d6. Hence White snaps it off forthwith: **1.Bxf5!**. (Fischer – Berliner, New York 1960)

(221)* Distant opposition
White splits the point by **1.Kg1**; for example, **1...Kf4** [or 1...f4 2.Kf2] **2.Kf2** and Black cannot make progress.

(222)*** Positional exchange sac
1...Rxe3! 2.fxe3 Nc5 3.Qc2 Re8 4.Rf3 Bh6 5.Qc3 Qe7. Black has excellent compensation for the exchange – he has a great outpost for his knight (which in turn secures his queenside pawns), and his long-range pieces converge on e3. In contrast, White's bishop is constrained by his own pawns, and his major pieces are not working well together. (Polugaevsky – Petrosian, Moscow 1983)

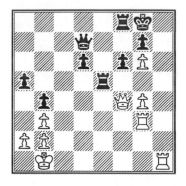

223. Black to move

226. White to move

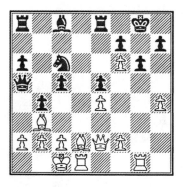

224. White to move

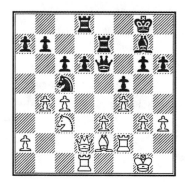

227. Black to move

225. White to move

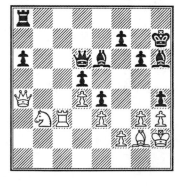

228. Black to move

(223)*** Stop threatened mate
Black must act upon the threat of 1.Rh8+! Kxh8 2.Rh3+ Kg8 3.Rh8+! Kxh8 4.Qh2+ Kg8 5.Qh7 mate. **1...Rfe8** is the best chance for survival. The Black king can escape via f8-e7, and the doubled rooks create opportunities for perpetual check.

(224)** Unstoppable force
1.Qh5!. The queen is heading toward h6 and g7. **1...Kh8** [1...Qd8 2.Rxg6+! Kh8 (2...hxg6 3.Qxg6+ with mate to follow) 3.Rg7 mating shortly; 1...Nd8 2.Qh6 Ne6 3.Bxe6 and it's mate next move] **2.Qh6** [2.Rxg6! also wins] **2...Rg8 3.Bxf7**. Black must jettison heavy material to stop imminent mate.

(225)** Pin, deflection, discovered attack
1.Bg5! Qf7 [or 1...Qg6 2.Be7 winning the exchange] **2.Bh6**. White wins material by capturing next on g7.

(226)*** Deflection, fork, avoid exchange
White has sacrificed a pawn for a massive lead in development. Rather than trade queens, White should play **1.Qc2!** preparing Rd1 followed by Qc6+. There is no defense: **1...Be7** allows the main idea [or 1...Bd7 2.Rb8+ Rxb8 3.Rxb8+ Ke7 4.Bc5+ Kf6 5.Bxf8 with a decisive advantage] **2.Rd1**, when Black must surrender his queen or lose a rook to Qc6+.

(227)* Fork
1...Bxc3 2.Qxc3 Ne4 wins the exchange.

(228)**** Improve worst piece
Black should improve his worst piece by **1...Bd7! 2.Qa5 Bb5**. He has thereby prevented the exchange of this bishop (following the anticipated Nc5), protected his a-pawn (thus freeing his rook to take part in the offense), slowed White's invasion of the queenside, and taken control of the f1 square (hence leaving White vulnerable along the f-file after the inevitable exchange on g3). Note that Black's other bishop is already doing good work: after the capture on g3, the e3 pawn will become a target. (Euwe – Boleslavsky, Zürich 1953)

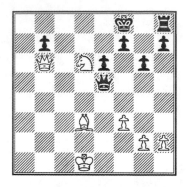

229. White to move

232. White to move

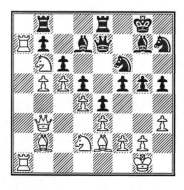

230. White to move

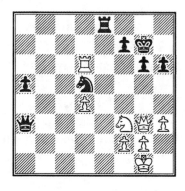

233. Black to move

231. White to move

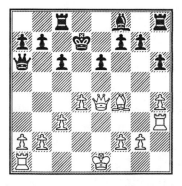

234. White to move

(229)** Decoy, fork
1.Qd8+ Kg7 2.Qxh8+! Kxh8 3.Nxf7+ clinches the full point.

(230)*** Skewer, overworked piece
The Black knight at f6 is strained, having to defend h5 and support d7. White takes advantage by **1.Nxd7 Nxd7** [1...Qxd7? 2.bxc6 Qxc6 (White emerges a full piece ahead after 2...bxc6 3.Rxd7 Rxb3 4.Rxg7+ Kxg7 5.Nxb3) 3.Bb5 skewering queen and rook] **2.Bxh5** winning a pawn.

(231)** Isolated passed pawns
1.g4!. If Black captures one pawn, then the other will promote, e.g., **1...Ke5 2.Ka2 Kf6 3.e4! Kg5 4.e5! Kg6 5.Ka3**, etc.

(232)** Double attack, remove the guard
1.Qb3!. Now White threatens to play Bxf7+, or win a piece by d4-d5 (hitting the defender of the b4 bishop). Black cannot meet both threats.

(233)** Fork, remove the guard, weak back rank
1...Nc3! wins, as White cannot meet the threat of ...Ne2+ and still defend his rook. For example, **2.Kf1 Ne2 3.Qh2? Qc1** mate.

(234)*** Impede enemy development
1.Be5! puts heat on the g7 pawn, thus interfering with Black's development. If Black tries ...f7-f6, then the weakened e6 pawn will become a juicy target. (Ponomariov – Conquest, Torshavn 2000)

235. Black to move

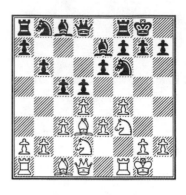

238. Black to move

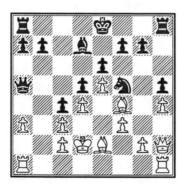

236. Black to move

239. Black to move

237. White to move

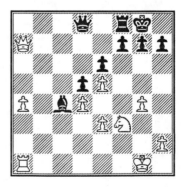

240. Black to move

(235)*** Eliminate opponent's best piece

Black enjoys a lead in development. In particular, his rooks are connected, sitting on useful files. Trading off White's best piece amplifies these advantages. **1...Nd7! 2.Nxd7** (forced, or else the b2 pawn is lost) **2...Rxd7**. All of Black's pieces are better placed than their counterparts. Next came **3.Bc1 Bc4!** once again removing White's best piece. **4.Rh3 Bxd3 5.Rxd3 Rxd3 6.cxd3 Rc2 7.Rb1 Bd4** winning a pawn. (Weiss – Blackburne, New York 1889)

(236)* Pin

1...Nxd4 wins a pawn.

(237)** Fast break

1.a5! is the only way to win. Any other move lets Black capture the e-pawn, then stop the queenside pawns. **1...Kxe5** [1...Kc5 2.b6 axb6 3.a6!] **2.b6 axb6 3.a6!** [not 3.axb6?? Kd6 drawing] and the pawn promotes.

(238)** Eliminate key piece

1...Ba6! eliminates the pride of White's position, his light-squared bishop, thus greatly reducing White's attacking prospects and further weakening the hole at e4.

(239)** Linear mate

Black is assured of delivering "linear mate" after **1...R8c5!** [1...R2c5! works equally well]. White has only desperation maneuvers, but these must be checked carefully, e.g., **2.dxc5 2...Rxc5 3.Be5 Rxe5 4.Rb5 Rxb5 5.Qf1 Rh5+ 6.Qh3 Rxh3** mate.

(240)**** Swap off vital defender

White has a passed pawn, but his king is exposed, and his queen cannot easily return for defense. Black takes charge by chopping off the defensive knight, allowing his queen to penetrate dangerously. **1...Be2! 2.Kf2 Bxf3! 3.Kxf3 Qh4** with tremendous counterplay.

92

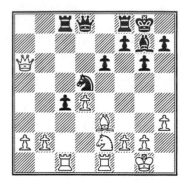

241. Black to move

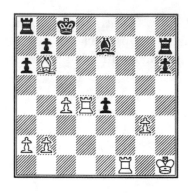

244. White to move

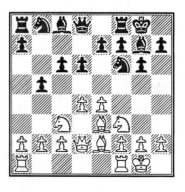

242. Black to move

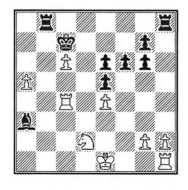

245. Black to move

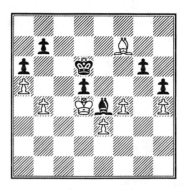

243. White to move

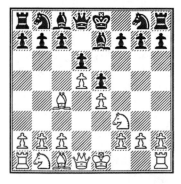

246. White to move

(241)* Fork
1...Nb4 2.Qb5 Nd3 wins the exchange.

(242)* Uneven trade
1...b4 2.Nd1 Nxe4 3.Qxb4. Black has advantageously traded his flank pawn for a White center pawn.

(243)*** Create passed pawn
1.f5! wins by creating a dangerous passed pawn. **1...Bxf5** [1...gxf5 2.Bxh5 gives White an outside passed pawn; 1...g5 2.hxg5 h4 3.g6 Bxf5 (3...h3 4.g7 h2 5.g8Q h1Q 6.Qd8+ White delivers mate next move) 4.g7 Bh7 5.Bxd5 and wins] **2.Bxd5 Bc8 3.e4**. Now with firm control of e5, White is winning. (Polugaevsky – Mecking, Mar del Plata 1971)

(244)* Deflection
1.Rf8+ Bxf8 2.Rd8 mate.

(245)*** Pin, skewer
1...Rb2!. The immediate threat is Bb4. **2.Kc2** [or else: 2.Nf3 Rb1+ wins a rook; 2.Kd1 Rd8 wins a piece; 2.Nf1 Bb4+ 3.Kd1 Rd8+ 4.Kc1 Ba3 with a deadly discovered check] **2...Bb4 3.Rd1 Rd8** and the defense crumbles.

(246)** Discourage enemy break
Never move the same piece twice in the opening...until it's a good move. **1.Bd3!** prevents Black from gaining space on the kingside by ...f7-f5, while clearing the way for his own queenside expansion by c2-c4. (Tarrasch – Showalter, Vienna 1898)

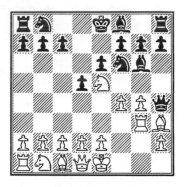

247. White to move

250. White to move

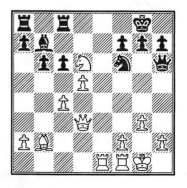

248. Black to move

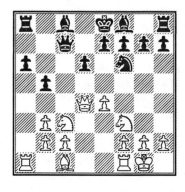

251. White to move

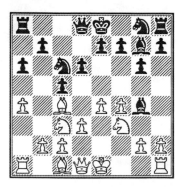

249. White to move

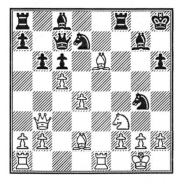

252. Black to move

(247)* Fork
1.Nf3 Qh6 2.g5 wins a piece.

(248)* Discovered attack
1...Ng4! threatens mate and opens up an attack on the d6 knight.
After **2.h4 Qxd6** Black is a clear piece to the good.

(249)* Discovered attack
1.Bxf7+! wins at least a pawn, since after **1...Kxf7** White regains
a piece by **2.Ng5+ Ke8 3.Qxg4**.

(250)*** Destroy counterplay
1.Bxe5?? loses to Rh4 mate. Instead, **1.Rg6!!** forces an exchange
of rooks, thus dashing Black's hopes for mate or perpetual check.
1...Rxg6 [or 1...Rh4+ 2.Kg3 Rg4+ 3.Rxg4 Rxg4+ 4.Kh3;
1...Rf2+ 2.Kg3 Rxg6+ 3.Kxf2] **2.Bxe5+ Kg8 3.Bxf4**. White's
unopposed central pawn mass seals the victory.

(251)** Pin, fork
White wins a clear pawn by **1.Nxb5!**, for if **1...Qxc2?** [worse is
1...axb5?? 2.Rxa8] **2.Qb6** the threat of Nc7+ is devastating.

(252)** Exchange sac
1...Rxf3! chops off the defender of h2. **2.gxf3** [2.Qxf3 Qxh2+
3.Kf1 Ba6+ also leads to mate] **2...Qxh2+ 3.Kf1 Qxf2** mate.

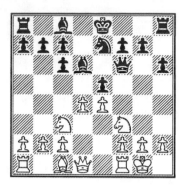

253. White to move

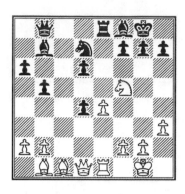

256. White to move

254. White to move

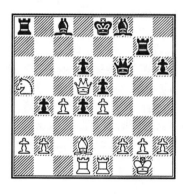

257. Black to move

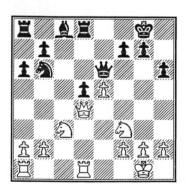

255. White to move

258. White to move

(253)** Pawn majority, bishop pair

1.dxe5! [1.Nxe5 first works equally well] **1...Bxe5 2.Nxe5 Qxe5.**
White has broken up his opponent's bishop pair, and established
a healthy kingside pawn majority.

(254)*** Create passed pawns

White wins by **1.Bxf6! gxf6 2.f4! Kd6 3.g5** creating a passed
pawn on the kingside, **3...fxg5 4.fxg5 Ke7 5.gxh6 Kf8 6.b4** and
another one on the queenside. Black cannot stop both.

(255)**** Remove the guard, create outpost

1.a4! threatens to remove a defender of d5, after which the
embattled pawn falls. If Black tries **1...a5** then White seizes the
newly created outpost by **2.Nb5** with a decisive advantage. For
example, **2...Qg6 3.Nc7 Rb8 4.e6!** (interference) **4...Na8 5.e7**
and wins.

(256)*** Double attack, pawn structure

1.Nh6+! gxh6 2.Qg4+ Kh8 3.Qxd7. White regains the piece,
after having wrecked the pawn cover for the Black king. (Fischer
– Keres, Zürich 1959)

(257)** The firstest with the mostest

1...Qf3! wins for Black. If 2.g3 Bh3 then Qg2 mate; 2.Kf1 Rxg2
3.Rc2 Rxh2 threatening Rh1 mate. White's desperation checks
also come to nothing.

(258)*** Trapped piece, pin

The Black knight is nearly trapped. White should start by
pinning its defender: **1.Ra3! Nc2 2.Ra2 a4 3.b4 a3 4.Ke2 Kf7
5.Kd2** and finally the horse is caught.

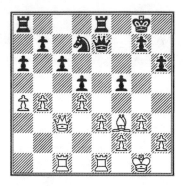

259. White to move

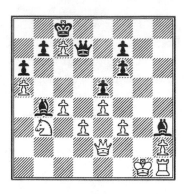

262. Black to move

260. White to move

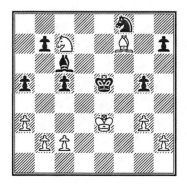

263. Black to move

261. White to move

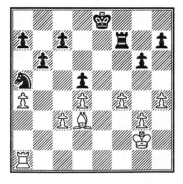

264. White to move

(259)*** Minority attack
By advancing the b-pawn, White will leave his opponent with a backward pawn on c6, or isolated pawns on d5 and b7: **1.b5! axb5 2.axb5 Rec8 3.bxc6 bxc6** [not 3...Rxc6?? 4.Bxd5+]. Now White has a tasty target on c6.

(260)** Double attack
1.Rxc6? Nc4+ 2.Kd5+ Rxc6 3.Kxc6 Nxa3 is bad for White. However, the intrepid **1.Kxc6!** wins at least a piece. Indeed, Black's discovered checks are harmless. For example, **1...Nc4+** [or 1...Kf5 2.Kb5; 1...Na8+ 2.Kb7] **2.Kb5** attacking knight and rook.

(261)* Fork, deflection
1.Nc6+! Bxc6 2.Qd8 mate.

(262)** Deflection, mate
1...Bc5+! deflects the White knight from defense of d5. **2.Nxc5** [2.d4 Bxd4+ 3.Nxd4 Qxd4+ 4.Qf2 Qa1+ 5.Qf1 Qxf1 mate; 2.Nd4 Qxd4+ 3.Qf2 Qxf2 mate] **2...Qd4+ 3.Qf2 Qa1+ 4.Qe1 Qxe1** mate.

(263)*** Trapped piece
The White knight is dangerously short of safe squares. **1...Kd6! 2.Na8** [2.Ne8+ Ke7 wins a piece] **2...Nd7** taking away the b6 square. Now the threat is ...b5. There followed **3.Bg8 h6 4.Bh7** (trying to get to e4) [another try is 4.c4 b5 5.Bd5 bxc4 6.Bxc6 Kxc6 7.Ke4 Kb7 and the horse is cornered anyway] **4...Nf6! 5.Bg6 Nd5+ 6.Kf3 b5** and at last the knight falls.

(264)*** Obtain rook on the 7th rank
1.h5! threatens to win a pawn, so Black's reply is forced. **1...Rf6** [1...gxh5 2.Rh1] **2.hxg6 hxg6 3.Rh1** followed by **4.Rh7**. The rook on the 7th rank attacks Black's pawns and limits the activity of Black's king. (Capablanca – Tartakower, New York 1924)

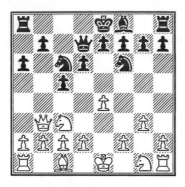

265. Black to move

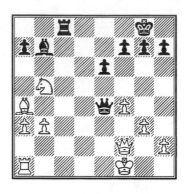

268. Black to move

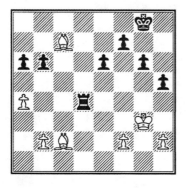

266. Black to move

269. White to move

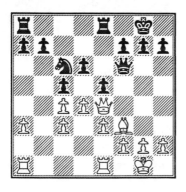

267. White to move

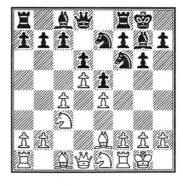

270. Black to move

(265)* Fork
1...Nd4 2.Qc4 [or 2.Qa4 Qxa4 3.Nxa4 Nxc2+] **2...Nxc2+.** Black
wins the exchange and stops White from castling.

(266)* Double attack
1...Rc4! picks off a bishop.

(267)*** Create and seize open file
White takes command by **1.dxc5!** [closing the center by 1.d5?
favors the side with the knight]. **1...dxc5 2.Rad1 Rad8 3.Rd5!**
b6 [3...Rxd5? 4.cxd5 would give White a protected passed
pawn] **4.Red1.** Now White owns the open file, and his bishop
has plenty of scope. (Botvinnik – Chekhover, Leningrad 1938)

(268)* Vulnerable king and queen
1...Rc2! forces White to give up his queen or get mated.

(269)** Positional pawn sac
1.d5! exd5 2.e5. White has blocked the enemy bishop and queen,
freed the lovely d4 square for his knight, and opened up the b1–
h7 diagonal for his bishop. (Polugaevsky – Tal, Moscow 1969)

(270)** Prepare pawn break
With the center pawns blocked, each player will seek activity in
the respective wing in which he has more space. Accordingly,
Black's plan is to launch a kingside pawn storm starting with
...f7-f5. First, he clears the way by **1...Nd7** [or ...Ne8].

271. Black to move

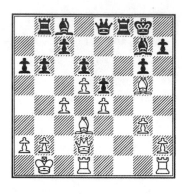

274. Black to move

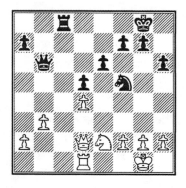

272. Black to move

275. White to move

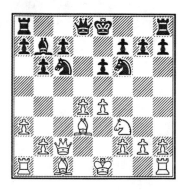

273. White to move

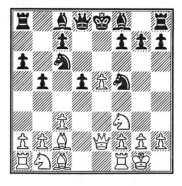

276. White to move

(271)* Vulnerable king
1...Qh5+ 2.Kg3 Qh4 mate.

(272)** Artificial support point
Black is in charge here, owning the c-file and bearing down on the isolated d-pawn. Now **1...h5!** discourages g2-g4, therefore securing the knight on f5. (White could dislodge the steed by 2.Ng3 Nxg3 3.hxg3, but at the cost of doubled pawns and weakening c3.) Now **2.h3** is met by **2...h4!**. (Em. Lasker – Capablanca, Havana 1921)

(273)* Pin
1.Bb5 wins material, e.g., **1...Qd7 2.Ne5 Nxe5 3.Bxd7+ Nexd7**.

(274)** Control open file
Black takes control of the open f-file by **1...Bh3!**, for then White's rooks will be unable to oppose Black's from f1. Trying to swap off the bishop doesn't help White: 2.Bf1 Bg4 3.Be2 Rf2!.

(275)** Cut off enemy king
1.Rg1+!. This forces the Black king offside, allowing White's king and pawns to advance in the center. **1...Kh6 2.e6!**. The resulting passed pawn secures the win.

(276)** Interference, deny castling
1.e6! interferes with the defense of the f5 knight. **1...Qf6** [1...Bxe6?? 2.Bxf5] **2.exf7+ Kxf7**. White has a clear positional advantage.

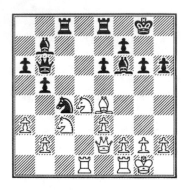

277. Black to move

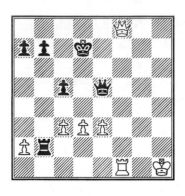

280. White to move

278. Black to move

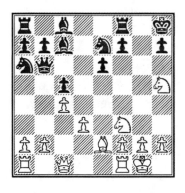

281. White to move

279. White to move

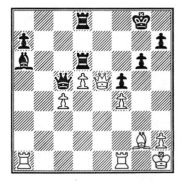

282. White to move

(277)*** Don't grab the pawn

In the game Black played **1...Bg7** tidying up his kingside. Indeed, Black must reject the tactical shot 1...Nxa3?? with the idea of winning a pawn by 2.bxa3?? 2...Rxc3. Instead, White has 2.Qf3! putting three Black pieces *en prise*. Black loses at least the exchange for a pawn: 2...Rxc3 [2...Bxe4 3.Nxe4 Bxd4 4.Rxd4 Nc4 5.Nf6+] 3.bxc3. (Grünfeld − Alekhine, Carlsbad 1923)

(278)* Philidor Review

After **1...Rb1!** the White king has no cover from endless checks, thus ensuring a draw. If he tries to "charge" the Black rook, then the pawn will fall.

(279)** Lucena Review

The enemy king has been cut off from the pawn. The next step is "building the bridge" by **1.Rc4!**. The White king will get out of the pawn's way and be shielded from checks at just the right time: **1...Rf2** [1...Re1 2.Rf4 Re2 3.Kf7 and Black must give up the rook or the pawn will promote] **2.Kd7 Rd2+ 3.Ke6 Re2+ 4.Kd6 Rd2+** [4...Kb6 5.Rd4 Re1 6.Kd7 winning] **5.Ke5 Re2+ 6.Re4**. The same idea with 1.Rc5 doesn't quite work, due to 1...Kb6.

(280)** Exposed king, skewer

1.Rf7+ Kc6 2.Qc8+ Kb6 [2...Kd5 3.Qd7+ Qd6 4.Rf5 mate] **3.Rxb7+** picks up the loose rook on b2.

(281)** Vulnerable king

1.Qh6 Rg8 [1...Qxb2 2.Ng5 followed by 3.Qxh7 mate] **2.Qf6+ Rg7 3.Qxg7** mate.

(282)**** Break the blockade

1.Rxa6! Rxa6 2.d6! Qxe5 [forced, or else 2...Qxd6? 3.Bd5+ Kf8 4.Qh8+ Ke7 5.Qg7+ Ke8 6.Qf7 mate] **3.fxe5**. In return for the exchange, White has obtained three advanced connected passed pawns. (Panov − Taimanov, Moscow 1952)

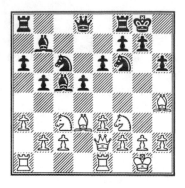

283. Black to move

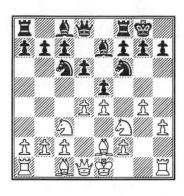

286. Black to move

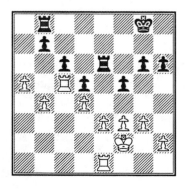

284. White to move

287. White to move

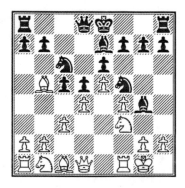

285. Black to move

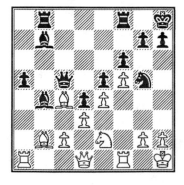

288. Black to move

(283)**** Win a piece, lose the game

Black can win a piece by 1...e5?, threatening to fork two pieces or chase the bishop on d3. But after 2.Bxf6! gxf6 [relatively better is 2...Qxf6 3.Nxd5 when Black has only lost a pawn] 3.Nh4 e4 4.Nxe4 dxe4 5.Qg4+ White has a devastating attack. Instead, Black would do better with **1...Be7** or **1...Rc8**.

(284)** Break up opposing pawn chain

White creates a passed pawn while leaving Black with weaknesses: **1.b5! Ra8** [1...cxb5 2.Rxd5 b4 3.Rb5; 1...Rbe8 2.bxc6 bxc6 3.a6] **2.bxc6 bxc6 3.Rb1** with a winning advantage.

(285)** Pressure weak pawn

1...cxd4 2.cxd4 Qb6 and the d4 pawn falls, e.g., **3.Bxc6+ bxc6 4.Kh1 Bxf3 5.Rxf3 Qxd4.**

(286)** Meet flank assault by central action

White has launched a flank attack while the center is fluid and his king is uncastled. Black rightly responds by a central thrust: **1...exd4! 2.Nxd4 d5!**. Black will clear the central files toward the White king well before White can break through on the kingside.

(287)** Anticipate tactical idea

The plausible move 1.Kd4? must be rejected because of the reply 1...Bxf3! when Black wins. Instead, securing f3 by **1.Bd1** is necessary to hold the draw.

(288)* Overworked piece

Black wins a pawn by **1...Nxe4!** since the d3 pawn is overworked. Note that 1...Bxe4? is inferior due to 2.h4 Nf7 3.Bxf7 Bxg2+ 4.Kxg2 Rxf7.

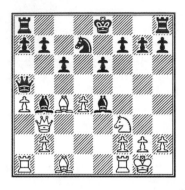

289. White to move

292. Black to move

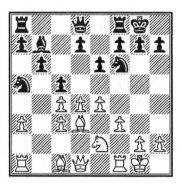

290. Black to move

293. White to move

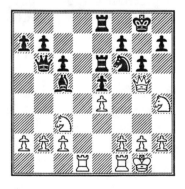

291. White to move

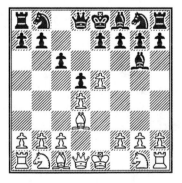

294. White to move

(289)*** Double attacks, deny castling
1.Bxe6! Bd5 [otherwise Black loses material: 1...0–0–0 2.Bxf7 Bxf3 3.Qxf3 Rhf8 4.Qb3; 1...fxe6 2.Qxe6+ Kf8 3.Qxe4; 1...Bxf3 2.Bxd7+ Kxd7 3.Qxf7+ Kc8 4.Qxf3] **2.Bxd5 cxd5 3.Qe3+ Kf8** and Black cannot castle [3...Be7? 4.Re1 is even worse].

(290)*** Prevent annoying pin
White is threatening Bg5 (with thoughts of e4-e5), when the pin cannot be broken without some kind of concession, such as weakening Black's kingside. By **1...Ne8!!** Black prevents the pin, and clears the way for his f-pawn to challenge White's broad pawn center. Later, the knight may head to d6, hitting the weak c4 pawn. (Geller – Euwe, Zürich 1953)

(291)*** Tempting line fails
The otherwise attractive move 1.Na4? is punished by 1...Bxf2+! 2.Kh1 [2.Rxf2 Qxf2+ 3.Kxf2 Nxe4+] 2...Nxe4 3.Nxb6 Nxg5 4.Rxf2 axb6. Rather, Black needs to bite the bullet and defend his b-pawn by **1.Rb1.**

(292)** Queen vs. pawn on the 7th rank
1...Qc6+! forces the White king to block his pawn's advance. Repeating this idea gives the Black king time to march toward the action. A typical finish is **2.Kd8 Kd5 3.Ke7 Qe6+ 4.Kd8 Kc6 5.Kc8 Qxd7+ 6.Kb8 Qb7.**

(293)* Stalemate trick
1.Ka8! frustrates Black's efforts due **1...Qxc7** stalemate.

(294)** Force weaknesses
White has a fine opportunity in **1.e6!** [or 1.Bxg6 first] **Qd6** [after 1...fxe6 2.Bxg6+ hxg6 3.Qd3 White will enjoy the lovely e5 outpost, and attack the targets on e6 and g6; the Black king is in for a long, cold winter after 1...Bxd3 2.exf7+ Kxf7 3.Qxd3] **2.exf7+ Bxf7 3.Nf3.** White will exploit the weak squares e5 and e6.

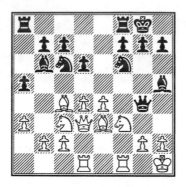

295. White to move

298. White to move

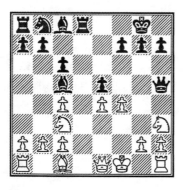

296. Black to move

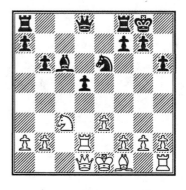

299. Black to move

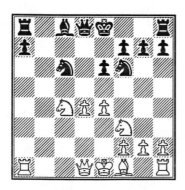

297. White to move

300. Black to move

(295)**** Vulnerable queen

The Black queen isn't threatening anything at the moment. **1.Bg5!** takes advantage of her exposed condition. The threat is to stick Black with doubled f-pawns, and there isn't a satisfactory answer. **1...Nd7?** doesn't help, as **2.h3 Qg3 3.Ne2** traps the Black queen. **1...Ne8** is just awful: the knight gets in the way and has no place to go. Allowing the exchange by **1...Rac8 2.h3 Qd7 3.Bxf6 gxf6 4.Nd5** and White is much better.

(296)* Vulnerable king

1...Bxh3 wins a piece, since **2.gxh3?** would allow **2...Qf3+** with mate next move.

(297)** Pin, outpost, prevent castling

White has two strong continuations. The simplest is **1.e5 Nd5 2.Nd6+** when Black has lost castling privileges, and White has a powerful knight on d6. Black's knight on d5 is not doing much, however. The alternative **1.Qa4** is also crushing: **1...Bd7** [**1...Qc7 2.e5 Nd5 3.Nd6+ Kf8 4.Rc1**; **1...Qd7 2.Na5**; **1...Bb7 2.e5 Nd5 3.Nd6+**] **2.Nd6+ Kf8 3.Bb5.**

(298)* Fork

1.c5 wins a piece.

(299)*** Positional pawn sac

After **1...d4! 2.exd4 Re8** White's pawn is blocking his own queen-rook battery and his king is staring at a nasty discovered check; meanwhile Black has opened up the long diagonal for his bishop. (Magerramov – Kasparov, Baku 1977)

(300)* Double attack

1...Be3 2.Qd3 Bxf4 wins back a pawn.

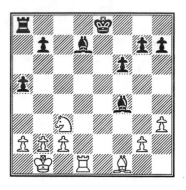

301. White to move

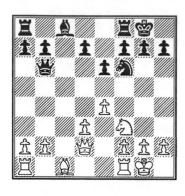

304. Black to move

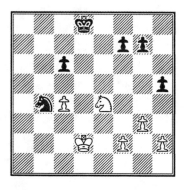

302. White to move

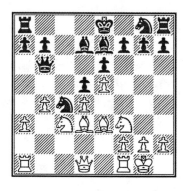

305. White to move

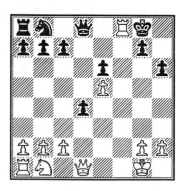

303. Black to move

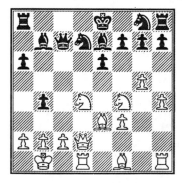

306. White to move

(301)** Fork, pin
1.Nd5! wins a piece, e.g., **1...Bg3 2.Nb6 Rd8 3.Rxd7 Rxd7 4.Bb5**.

(302)** Trapped piece
1.Nc5!. This controls a6 and d3, potential flight squares for the Black knight. **1...Kc7 2.Kc3 Na2+ 3.Kb2 Nb4 4.Kb3**. The knight is trapped.

(303)** Pawn weaknesses
Which recapture? 1...Kxf8 holds on to d4, but allows 2.Qf3+ Kg8 3.Qxb7. After saving the rook Black has loose pawns to worry about. Better is **1...Qxf8 2.Qxd4 Nc6 3.Qc3 Qf5** when it is White who will drop a pawn.

(304)*** Development, center
Black has to attend to two matters: get his bishop into play, and grab a share of the center. By **1...d6 2.b3 e5** Black's bishop is freed, and White is prevented from expanding by e4-e5. The "hole" on d5 is not a worry, as White is not in a position to occupy it.

(305)** Discovered attack, space, development
1.Bxc4! dxc4 **2.d5** (discovered attack) **2...Qa6 3.d6 Bd8**. White enjoys a huge space advantage and a lead in development.

(306)*** Uncastled king, loose material
White wins by **1.Ndxe6!** [1.Nfxe6 is equally effective] **1...fxe6 2.Nxe6 Qc6 3.Nxg7+ Kf8** [3...Kd8 4.Bh3] **4.Qxd7**. White has regained the invested piece, and the attack rages on. Note that 4...Kxg7 is met by **5.Bd4+** snaring a rook.

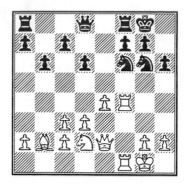

307. White to move

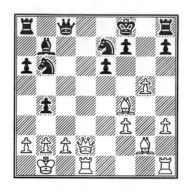

310. White to move

308. Black to move

311. White to move

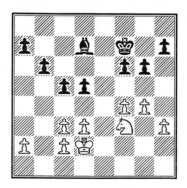

309. Black to move

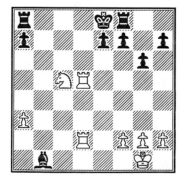

312. White to move

(307)** Exchange sac yields attack

The position begs for the exchange sacrifice **1.Rxf6! gxf6 2.Qh5 Kh7**. White could follow up with **3.Bc1!**, Nd2-c4-e3-f5, and Rf1-f3-h3 with a winning attack.

(308)*** Take the short side

Due to the threat of mate, the Black king must abandon the promotion square [note that 1...Re1? loses to 2.Ra8+ Re8 3.Rxe8+ Kxe8 4.Kg7]. The rule of thumb here is that the defending king should run to the "short" side: **1...Kg8! 2.Ra8+ Kh7 3.Rf8 Ra1!** [indeed, going to the "long" side loses: 1...Ke8? 2.Ra8+ Kd7 3.Rf8 Rh1 4.Kf7 Rh7+ 5.Kg6 Rh1 6.f6 Rg1+ 7.Kf7]. Now Black draws by giving endless rook checks from the long side. Or, if White tries **4.Re8**, then Black goes back to **4...Rf1!**, and White has not made progress.

(309)*** Tie down enemy piece

White does not have a good answer to **1...h5! 2.Nh2** tying down the knight to the protection of g4 [2.gxh5 gxh5 3.Ng1 is also no good (here note that 3.h4 would allow the Black king to penetrate to f5 and g4)].

(310)* Double attack

1.Qd4! attacks the loose material on b6 and h8.

(311)** Pin, fork

1.c4! wins a piece, because **1...Nf6** [or 1...Nxe3 2.Bxc6+ Bd7 (2...Kf8 3.Rd8 mate) 3.Bxd7+ Kf8 4.fxe3] **2.Bxc6+ Bd7 3.Bxa8** would drop a whole rook.

(312)** Mate, fork

1.Na6 threatens Nc7, either winning the exchange or mating: **1...f6** [after 1...e6? 2.Rd7 Black loses a whole rook; 1...Rc8?? 2.Nc7+ Rxc7 3.Rd8 mate] **2.Nc7+ Kf7 3.Nxa8**.

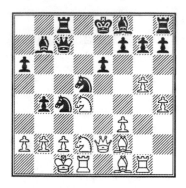

313. Black to move

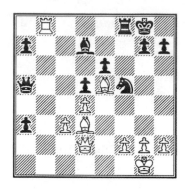

316. White to move

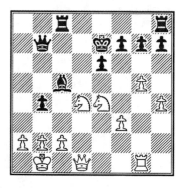

314. White to move

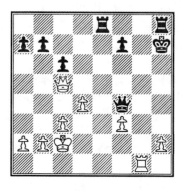

317. White to move

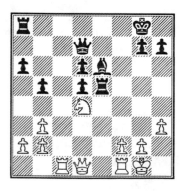

315. White to move

318. White to move

(313)** Piece sac for attack
Black secures the full point by 1...Nxb2! 2.Kxb2 Qc3+ 3.Kb1 Qa3 when there is no satisfactory defense against Nc3+.

(314)**** Open file, fork, trapped piece
White wins by 1.Nf5+!! ripping open the e-file. 1...exf5 [1...Kf8 loses a piece to 2.Nxc5 due to 2...Rxc5?? 3.Qd8 mate; 1...Ke8?? loses the queen after 2.Ned6+ Bxd6 3.Nxd6+] 2.Nxc5 Qc6 [2...Rxc5?? loses to 3.Re1+] 3.Rc1+ Kf8 4.Nd7+ Kg8 5.h5!. Now White is effectively playing a piece up, as the h8 rook will not see daylight for a very long time.

(315)*** Prevent counterattack
Black has ideas about 1...Bxh3 2.gxh3 Qxh3 with an attack or perpetual check. 1.Rc3 puts an end to such thoughts, and prepares to double rooks on the open c-file. (Ponomariov – Korchnoi, Donetsk 2001)]

(316)**** Remove key defender
1.Bxf5!! wins by removing the piece defending g7. White can meet any threats to his own back rank. 1...exf5 [1...Rxb8 2.Qg5 Kf7 3.Qxg7+ Ke8 4.Bf6 and Black has only spite checks left; 1...a2 2.Qg5 a1Q+ 3.Bb1 g6 4.Qe7 Qxb1+ 5.Rxb1 Rf7 6.Rb8+ mating] 2.Qg5 Kf7 3.Qxg7+ Ke6 4.Rxf8 with mate next move.

(317)* Unsafe king
1.Qh5+ Qh6 2.Qxf7+ Qg7 3.Qxg7 mate.

(318)*** No time for greed
The materialistic 1.Bxh3 Qxh3 2.Nxb7? invites trouble: 2...Ng4 3.Nf3 Nde3! 4.fxe3 Nxe3 5.Qxf7+ Kh8 (5...Kxf7?? 6.Ng5+) 6.Nh4 Rf8 and the White queen is pinned against mate at f1. White should prefer to preserve his light-squared bishop by 1.Bf3. (Réti – Alekhine, Baden-Baden 1925)

319. Black to move

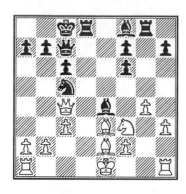

322. Black to move

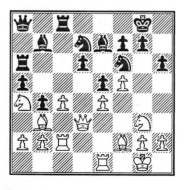

320. Black to move

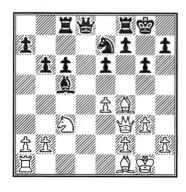

323. Black to move

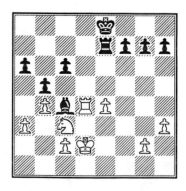

321. Black to move

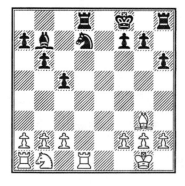

324. White to move

(319)** Rescue attacked piece
Each player has a rook *en prise*. Black gets his own rook out of danger by **1...Rd2+ 2.Kc6 Rc4+ 3.Kb7** allowing **3...Bxe1**.

(320)** Remove defender of weak squares
By **1...Ng4!** intending ...Nxf2 next, Black will not only obtain the bishop pair, but also remove the defender of the vulnerable dark squares in the White camp. (Anand – Ivanchuk, Linares 1991)

(321)* Vulnerable pawns
White's kingside pawns cannot be defended within a move. Black will surely win a pawn after **1...Bf1**.

(322)** Trapped piece
The White queen is lost after **1...b5! 2.Qb4 a5**. Alternatively, Black wins a piece by 1...Bd5 2.Qf4 Qxf4 3.Bxf4 Bxf3 4.Bxf3 Nd3+.

(323)*** Defuse multiple threats
Black is up the exchange and a pawn, but White has the threat of 1.Ba6 Ra8 2.Bb7 regaining the exchange, and of Bh6 in conjunction with Rd1 or Qf6. **1...Qd4** defends the kingside dark squares, and vacates a square for the endangered c8 rook.

(324)*** Make the tactical idea work
1.Bc7? attacking the guard of d7 doesn't win material, as Black can respond 1...Rc8 2.Rxd7 Ke8 regaining the piece. However, **1.Bd6+!** nets at least the exchange: **1...Kg8** [1...Ke8 2.Re1+] **2.Be7**.

325. White to move

328. Black to move

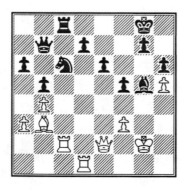

326. White to move

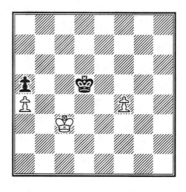

329. White to move

327. White to move

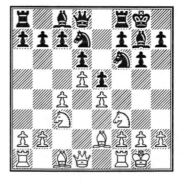

330. Black to move

(325)* Stop freeing move

1.Ne3! is best, preventing ...d6-d5(+), and thus keeping the Black bishop boxed in. 1.Nf6 is less clear: 1...Be7 2.Nd5 Bxg5 3.Nc7+ Kd7 4.Nxb5 Kc6.

(326)* Double attack, decoy, remove the guard

1.Rxd7! Qa8 [1...Qxd7 loses the queen to 2.Bxe6Ι] **2.Qxe6Ι** is crushing.

(327)**** Pin, deflection

1.Bh6!! deflects the defender of e5. Black loses at least a pawn: **1...Bxh6** [1...0–0 2.Bxg7 Kxg7 3.Nxe5 followed by capturing on d7; 1...Bf6 2.Bg5 Bg7 3.Nd5! and the e7 knight drops] **2.Nxe5**. Now the bishop on d7 falls. **2...Nc6 3.Nxd7**.

(328)** *Zugzwang*, same-colored bishops

1...Bg7! [or 1...Bh8!] **2.Be1 Be5**. White is in *zugzwang*: If he moves his bishop, then he loses a pawn; if he moves his king, then the Black king invades decisively.

(329)** Opposition, outside passed pawn

1.f5?? actually makes Black's defensive job easier, as he can now eat the f-pawn, and then scurry over to the corner to prevent the a-pawn from promoting. The only winning move for White is **1.Kd3!** taking the opposition. **1...Kc5** [on 1...Ke6 2.Kc4 Kf5 3.Kb5 Kxf4 4.Kxa5 Ke5 5.Kb6 Kd6 6.Kb7 White reaches g7 just in time to take control of the corner squares] **2.Ke4 Kd6 3.Kf5 Ke7 4.Kg6**. White has reached one of the "key squares" for his passed pawn, enabling it to promote.

(330)** Artificial support point

The c5 square is not a "hole" in the strict sense, as it can be attacked by a pawn. Yet, Black has **1...Nc5!** (now e4 is attacked) **2.Qc2 a5!** creating an "artificial support point" by inhibiting b2-b4. Note also that **3.a3**, intending b2-b4 later, can be answered by **3...a4!**.

331. White to move

334. White to move

332. White to move

335. White to move

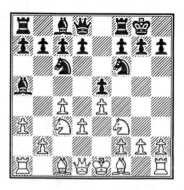

333. White to move

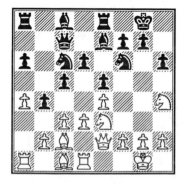

336. Black to move

(331)*** Interference, deflection, open file

1.Qh8+? Rg8 2.Qh6+ is a perpetual check at best. White should play **1.e4!** (interfering with Black's mating threat) **1...Bxe4** (the f-file is thus cleared for a decisive check) [1...dxe4 2.Rhf1 Qd7 3.Bg4] **2.Qh8+ Rg8 3.Rhf1+** winning.

(332)*** Mate, skewer

White wins with **1.Qf6!** threatening mate by Qh8+ (also skewering the a8 rook), while maintaining the pressure on e7. **1...Rxe1+ 2.Rxe1 Kg8 3.Re7**. Now Black must surrender his queen or be mated, e.g., **3...Qc1+ 4.Kh2 Rf8 5.Re3 Rc8** [5...Qc7+ 6.Rg3+] **6.Rg3+ Kf8 7.Qd6+ Ke8 8.Rg8** mate.

(333)* Trapped piece

1.b4 Bb6 2.c5 wins a piece.

(334)*** Endgame with rook and pawns

The routine exchange 1.exf6+ Kxf6 still leaves a lot of work to be done. Instead, White should play **1.Rc7+ Kf8 2.Rb7! fxe5** [2...Rxb3 is met by 3.a5! Ra3 4.axb6 Rb3 5.exf6 winning] **3.Rxb6** obtaining connected passed pawns.

(335)*** Win a pawn, lose the game

1.Qc4 maintains the balance. Indeed, White should resist snatching a pawn by 1.Rxe7? Rxe7 [1...Bxe7?? 2.Qxf7+] 2.Qxb8 as Black has the refutation 2...Re1+ 3.Rxe1 Qxe1+ 4.Kh2 Be5+ bagging the queen.

(336)** Beware the intermediate move

1...Nxe4? 2.dxe4? Bxh4 would win a pawn for Black, but White wins with the intermediate move 2.Nd5! Nxc3 (2...Qd8 3.Nxe7+ Qxe7 4.Qxe4) 3.bxc3 Qb7 4.Nxe7+ netting a piece for two pawns. Black should prefer **1...Be6** instead.

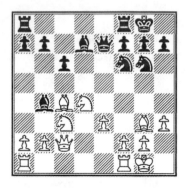

337. Black to move

340. White to move

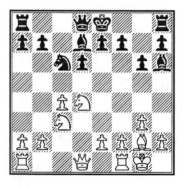

338. White to move

341. Black to move

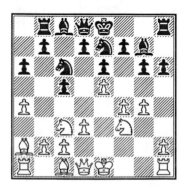

339. Black to move

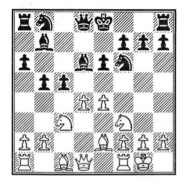

342. White to move

(337)**** Pawn structure, control center square
1...Bxc3!! sticks White with an unpleasant choice. 2.Qxc3 Ne4 3.Qd3 Nxg3 4.fxg3 and White's pawn structure is inferior. Or, **2.bxc3 2...Ne4 3.Bh2 c5 4.Nf3 Bc6** leaves White with a weak c-pawn and gives Black control of e4. Furthermore, if White tries to evict the knight by a later f2-f3, then his king position will be weakened, especially the surrounding dark squares. (Gligorić – Smyslov, Amsterdam 1971)

(338)**** Create target
1.c5!! dxc5 (otherwise White captures on d6, leaving Black with an isolated pawn) **2.Nxc6 Bxc6 3.Bxc6+ bxc6 4.Qc2**. Black is left with doubled isolated pawns on a semi-open file. White can recapture one pawn easily (thereby restoring the material balance), and then torment the other one mercilessly. (Andersson – Van der Wiel, Wijk aan Zee 1983)

(339)** Prevent positional threat
White has the positional threat of Nc3-e4-d6(+). Black can best address this by either **1...d6** or 1...d5. Black is fine after **2.exd6 Qxd6 3.Ne4 Qc7**. Note that the c5 pawn is safe: 4.Nxc5?? Qa5+.

(340)* Final king-hunt
1.Qh8+ Kg6 2.Rxg7+ Kf6 3.Qf8 mate.

(341)*** King position, reserve tempo
1...Ke6! is the winning move [1...h6? squanders a precious reserve tempo, allowing a draw: 2.Kg3 Kf5 3.Kf3 h5 4.a4; 1...dxc4?? throws away a full point, as White has the passed pawn after 2.bxc4]. **2.Kg3** [2.Kg5 d4! 3.Kg4 dxe3 4.Kf3 Kf5 5.Kxe3 Kg4 6.Ke4 Kxh4 the outside passed pawn decides; 2.a4 burns White's reserve tempo 2...Kf6 and now the White king must give way] **2...Kf5 3.Kf3 h6** [3...d4? 4.exd4 cxd4 5.b4!] **4.a4 h5** and now the Black king penetrates via e4 or g4.

(342)* Fork
1.e5 wins a piece.

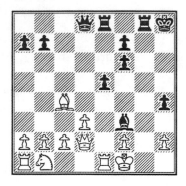

343. Black to move

346. White to move

344. Black to move

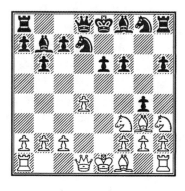

347. White to move

345. Black to move

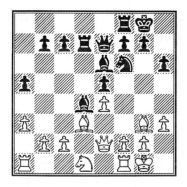

348. White to move

(343)** Clearance
1...Rg1+!! 2.Kxg1 Rg8+ 3.Kf1 [3.Qg5 doesn't save White]
3...Rg1+ 4.Kxg1 Qg8+ 5.Kf1 Qg2 mate.

(344)** Clearance, pin
At the moment White has three advanced center pawns for a
piece. **1...Nxe6!** eats one pawn and clears c5 for the bishop. The
knight is safe, as **2.dxe6? Bc5** wins the queen.

(345)* Double attack
1...Nxh4! simply wins a pawn, as after **2.Bxh4?** Black wins
another pawn and regains the piece by **2...Rxf4**, hitting both
bishops.

(346)*** Pin, weak back rank, fork, defense
1.Qd4! wins material. It also prevents Black's intended ...Nf4
and ...Qh3+. If Black defends the e5 knight, for instance by
1...Qd6, then **2.Rce1**. Moving the knight is no better: 1...Nf7
2.Qxd5! Qd8 (Black's weak back rank must be held) 3.Rxe8+
Qxe8 4.Re1 Qf8 5.Qd7 with the double threat of Re8 and Qxh3;
1...Nc6 (or ...Nc4) loses to 2.Rxe8+ Qxe8 3.Qxd5+.

(347)*** Rescue attacked pieces
White rescues his knights by **1.Nh4!** followed by Nf4, the
tactical point being that **1...gxh3? 2.Qh5+ Ke7 3.Ng6+** wins,
e.g., **Kf7 4.Ne5+ Ke7 5.Qf7+ Kd6 6.Nc4+ Kc6 7.Qxe6+ Kb5
8.Nd6+ Ka5 9.Nxb7+ Ka4 10.Qb3** mate.

(348)*** Don't snatch the pawn
Black enjoys superior development and an equal share of the
center. Furthermore, he is about to double rooks on the only
open file. Accordingly, White must resist grabbing a pawn by
1.c3? Ba7 2.Bxe5 as this weakens the d-file irreparably. Black
enjoys terrific compensation: 2...Rfd8 3.Bxf6 [3.Bc2? drops the
bishop to 3...Rd2; 3.Bb1 Rd2 is miserable for White; 3.Bb5 loses
to 3...c6 4.Ba4 b5 as the bishop has no place to go] 3...Qxf6 4.e5
Qg5 5.Be4 Bxh3. A more prudent course for White would be
1.Rb1 Rfd8 2.Ne3, getting the knight back into play.

349. Black to move

352. Black to move

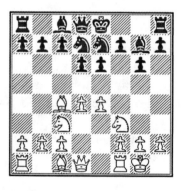

350. White to move

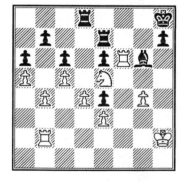

353. White to move

351. White to move

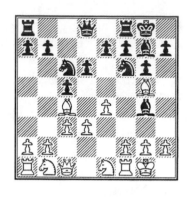

354. White to move

(349)**** Attack, safety net
Black's d-pawn is under attack. The solid 1...Qe7 would be enough to preserve Black's material advantage. Better, however, is **1...Rxh2+!! 2.Kxh2 Rh8+ 3.Kg3 Nh5+ 4.Kh2** [4.Kg4 allows the Black queen to join in with check, and mate to follow: 4...Qd7+ 5.Kh4 Qe7+ 6.Kg4 (6.Kh3 Nf4+ 7.Kg4 f5+ 8.Kg3 Qh4 mate) 6...f5 ׀ 7.Kh3 Nf4 ׀ 8.Kg3 Qh4 mate] **4...Nf4׀ 5.Kg3** Black should have noted that at this point he has at least a perpetual check by ...Nh5+. Assuming that a draw would be acceptable, Black can proceed with the initial rook sacrifice without having to calculate beyond this point. Then he should look for a winning continuation. As it happens, Black does have a forced win, e.g., **5...Qe7! 6.Kf2 Rh2 7.Qf1 Qh4+ 8.Ke3 Nxg2+ 9.Kd3 Qd4+ 10.Kc2 Ne3+ 11.Kb3 Nxd1 12.Qxd1 Rb2+!.**

(350)** Obstruct enemy plans
The routine 1.Be3 would be just fine, but **1.a4!** better meets the demands of the position. This move discourages Black from the queenside fianchetto (i.e.,...b6 followed by ...Bb7) – where will he put that bishop now? It also stops Black from expanding by ...a7-a6 [or ...c7-c6] and ...b7-b5. (Alekhine – Mikenas, Folkestone 1933)

(351)** Pin, trapped piece
1.Bh6! wins material, since **1...Rf7** meets with **2.Qe3** trapping the h3 bishop.

(352)* Trapped piece
1...Be2 picks up the exchange.

(353)* Pin
White wins back a piece by **1.Rxe4! Rxe4 2.Bd3**.

(354)** Fork, desperado
White obtains a winning endgame by **1.Rxg6! hxg6 2.Nxg6+ Kg7 3.Nxe7 Re8 4.Nxc6 bxc6 5.Kg3**. 1.Nxg6+ hxg6 2.Rxg6 e5 3.dxe5 Rxe5 leaves White with a more difficult technical task.

355. White to move

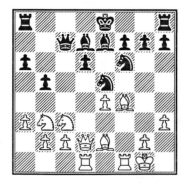

358. White to move

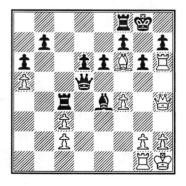

356. Black to move

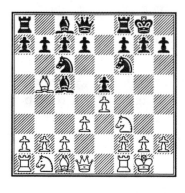

359. White to move

357. White to move

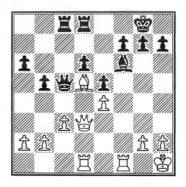

360. Black to move

(355)**** Local superiority of force
White would have the edge after 1.Qg3. However, **1.Rxf6! gxf6 2.Qf3!** is completely winning [2.Qg3+? would give Black an extra tempo to organize a defense: 2...Kh8 3.Qh4 Rg8 4.Qxf6+ Rg7 5.Rf1 Qc7 and holds]. Black's queen and rooks just can't cover the exposed lines in time. The finish could be **2...Rc7 3.Qxf6 Rdd7 4.Rd3 Kf8 5.Rg3 Qa7 6.Bxf7 Rxf7 7.Qd8** mate.

(356)*** Defense, double attack
Black not only defends against the mating threats, but also obtains a decisive advantage, by **1...Bxg2+! 2.Rxg2 Qd1+ 3.Rg1 Qf3+ 4.Rg2 Rxf4** attacking the bishop and queen. Black's extra pawns will decide.

(357)** Same-colored bishops, promotion
1.Bc2 (1.Ba4 Bh5 2.Bc2 Be8 amounts to the same thing) **1...Ke5 2.Bg6.** Black must yield c7, and then the pawn cannot be stopped.

(358)*** Pawn sac for active king
1.f5! [1.Kf3 followed by 2.Rg3 is less clearly winning] **1...exf5 2.Kf4.** White regains the pawn with excellent piece placement. The finish was **2...Re6** [also futile is 2...Rf7 3.Rg3+ Kh6 4.Rg5] **3.Kxf5 Rg6 4.e6! Rg4 5.Ke5 Re4+ 6.Kd6 Rxd4 7.Re3.** (Capablanca – Eliskases, Moscow 1936)

(359)* Remove the guard
White can safely snatch a pawn by **1.Bxc6 dxc6 2.Nxe5**.

(360)** Blunder check
The natural 1...0–0?? is punished by 2.Bxe5 dxe5 3.Rxf6! Bxf6 4.Qxd7 when White nabs two pieces for a rook. Instead, Black should prefer **1...Nc4 or 1...Be6.**

361. Black to move

364. White to move

362. White to move

365. White to move

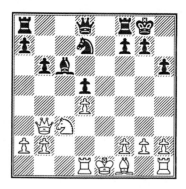

363. Black to move

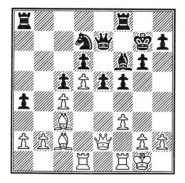

366. Black to move

(361)*** Deflection
Black is a clear pawn up after **1...cxd4 2.Nxd4 Nfxd4 3.exd4 Nxd4!** since **4.Qxd4??** drops material to the deflection **4...Re1+! 5.Rxe1** [5.Bf1 Qxd4 6.Rxd4 Rxa1] **5...Qxd4.**

(362)*** Force a second weakness
White will already be targeting Black's isolated d-pawn. By **1.b4!** White fixes an enemy pawn on a6, and prepares to attack it by Nc5. Note that **1...a5** would allow **2.b5**, when the passed pawn is even more of a problem for Black. (Fischer – Petrosian, Buenos Aires 1971)

(363)** Hold back enemy development
1...Qg5! ties the White bishop down to the defense of g2, and thus keeps the White king stuck in the central files. 1...Re8+ 2.Be2 Qg5 achieves the same thing.

(364)** Discovered attack
1.Rxe6! wins a piece, due to the combination **1...fxe6 2.Bxe6+ Kf8 3.Rxd8+.**

(365)** Guard against double attack
Black is threatening to win the exchange by ...cxd4 followed by ...Bc4. **1.Rfd1** solves the problem.

(366)*** Positional pawn sac
1...e4! 2.Bxf6+ [2.fxe4 Bxc3 3.bxc3 f4 is similar] **2...Qxf6 3.fxe4 f4!.** In return for a pawn, Black has a good knight versus White's bad bishop; in addition, his kingside pawn majority is looking ominous. (Pilnik – Geller, Göteborg 1955)

367. Black to move

370. Black to move

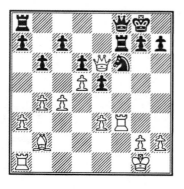

368. Black to move

371. White to move

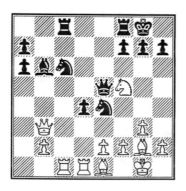

369. White to move

372. White to move

(367)** Exchange sac for attack
1...Rxf3! 2.gxf3 Nxe5. Black will get a pawn and a promising attack for the exchange.

(368)*** Force advantageous queen swap
1...Qc8! forces the exchange of queens, leaving White unable to guard e4. After **2.Qxc8+ Rxc8** the Black knight will head for the newly created e4 outpost, from where it will strike deep into enemy territory, and from where it cannot be expelled. It also fixes the White pawn on e3, thereby boxing in the White bishop. (Nikolić – Timman, Amsterdam 1984)

(369)**** Pin, deflection, fork, remove the guard
The game went 1.Bxc4 Qxc4 2.Nd6 Qxe2 3.Nxc8, winning the exchange but losing his e2 pawn. White should have preferred **1.Qf3!**, still winning at least the exchange, while holding on to e2. **1...Nf6** [1...Nc5 2.b4 Nd7 3.Qf4 Qxe2 4.Qg5 g6 5.Bxc6 Rxc6 6.Ne7+; 1...Ng5 2.Qf4 Qf6 3.Nd6] **2.Qf4 Qxf4 3.gxf4.** White either wins the knight on c6, or delivers a nasty fork at e7. (Em. Lasker – Tarrasch, St. Petersburg 1914)

(370)** Make way for the mortal blow
1...Qd1+ 2.Rg1 Qd5+ 3.Rg2 Rf1 mate.

(371)*** Attack weak square
1.Bxc6! is best, clearing the g-file with tempo for an attack on g7. After **1...Rxc6 2.Rxc6 bxc6 3.Rg1 Qd5+ 4.Qxd5 Nxd5 5.Rxg7 Rb8 6.Be5**, White will pick off at least two pawns.

(372)* Remove the guard
1.Rxd5! wins a piece, as suddenly the Black queen is hanging.

373. Black to move

376. Black to move

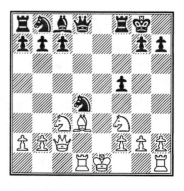

374. White to move

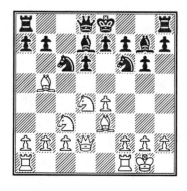

377. Black to move

375. Black to move

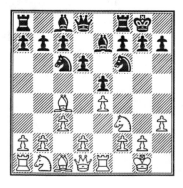

378. Black to move

(373)** Hold up enemy progress
1...Nd4! immobilizes White's queenside pawns and slows the White king's progress toward the center. (Smyslov – Sax, Tilburg 1979)

(374)* Discovered attack
White wins a piece by **1.Bc4+ Kh8 2.Nxd4.**

(375)** Vulnerable king
1...Qe3+ forces mate: **2.Kf1** [2.Kd1 Rb1+ 3.Kc2 Qb3 mate] **2...Rb1+ 3.Rd1 Rxd1+ 4.Qe1 Rxe1** mate.

(376)* Pin, doubled rooks
1...Rbb1 wins heavy material.

(377)* Bishop pair
Black should lop off the e3 bishop by **1...Ng4!**. This not only gives Black the bishop pair, but also enhances the value of his own dark-squared bishop.

(378)** Center fork trick
1...Nxe4!. Either Black remains a pawn up, or following **2.Rxe4 d5 3.Re1 dxc4 4.Nxe5 Nxe5 5.Rxe5 Bd6 6.Re3 Bf5**, Black has the bishop pair, a huge development lead, and a death-grip on the d3 square.

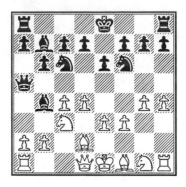

379. White to move

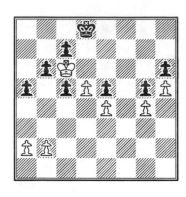

382. White to move

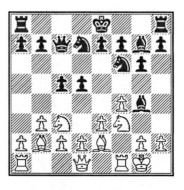

380. White to move

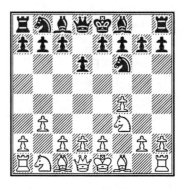

383. Black to move

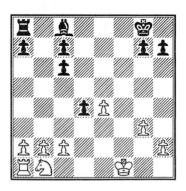

381. Black to move

384. White to move

(379)*** Nearly trapped piece

White wins due to the vulnerable position of the Black queen. **1.a3! Bxc3** [or 1...Bd6 (threatening ...Bg3+) 2.Rh3! Bc8 (2...Ne7 3.b4 Qa6 4.c5) 3.b4 Qa6 4.b5] **2.Bxc3 Qa6 3.c5 b5 4.a4 Ne7** [4...Bc8 5.axb5] **5.Bxb5** and now Black must give up a piece to rescue his queen **5...Bxf3! 6.Qxf3 Qc8**.

(380)* Pin

1.Nxd5 wins a pawn, as its putative defender is suddenly pinned.

(381)** Multi-purpose move

1...Rb8! compels the reply **2.b3**. Thus Black develops a piece with gain in time, prevents Nb1-d2-b3(-c5), and forces another enemy pawn onto the same color square as his bishop. (Marshall – Em. Lasker, New York 1907)

(382)** Undermine pawn chain

White has sacrificed a pawn for excellent king position. To finish the job: **1.d6! cxd6 2.Kxd6 Kc8 3.Kc6**. White will annihilate Black's queenside pawns for an easy win.

(383)*** Double attack, pawn center

1...e5! is good for Black, taking advantage of the momentary exposure of the a1 rook. For example, **2.fxe5** [2.e4 exf4 gives White an inferior King's Gambit – the c1 bishop eventually has to capture on f4, so b2-b3 was a wasted move; other tries such as 2.e3 allow 2...e4 3.Nd4 d5 when Black has a strong two-pawn center] **2...dxe5** gives Black free and easy development, because **3.Nxe5??** loses a piece to **3...Qd4**.

(384)*** Avoid the skewer

Perfunctory development such as 1.Be3? would allow 1...c5 2.Nf3 Bb5 skewering the queen and rook. Note that 3.c4?? doesn't help, due to 3...Bxh2+. Instead, White should play **1.Nf3** or **1.Nf5**.

385. Black to move

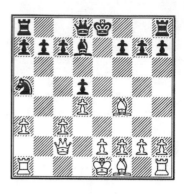

388. Black to move

386. White to move

389. White to move

387. Black to move

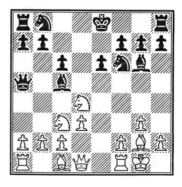

390. White to move

(385)*** Loose pieces
Black can win material, seeing that neither White minor piece
has a lot of safe squares. **1...c5! 2.Nb3** [2.Nb5 c6 and the knight
is trapped; 2.Nc6 Qd6 3.Na5 c4! and again the knight is doomed]
2...c4! 3.Nc1 [3.Nd4 c5 is a familiar story 4.Nc6 (4.Nb5 a6)
4...Qc7] **3...Rb8 4.Rb1 Bg4 5.Qe3 Rb6** intending ...Qb8,
winning the bishop. Resistance is futile, e.g., **6.Na2 Qb8 7.Nb4
a5**.

(386)** Is it really a threat?
In the actual game White played the undeveloping move 1.Bf1?
reacting to a non-existent threat. Something ordinary such as
1.Bg5 turns out to be just fine, as Black has no attack after
1...Bxh3?? 2.gxh3 Qxh3 3.Bf1 Qg4+ 4.Bg2.

(387)** Rook vs. two advanced pawns
Connected pawns on the 6th rank can usually beat a lone rook,
but here Black holds a trump card: **1...Rc1! 2.Kh3** (forced, due
to the threat of mate) **2...Rh1+ 3.Kg2 Rxh6 4.g7 Rg6+**.

(388)*** Disrupt enemy development
Castling now would allow White to play e2-e3 and complete his
development without difficulty. It is worth the tempo to play
1...Bb5!. If White tries e2-e3, then Black will capture on f1,
preventing White from castling. If White goes for the fianchetto,
then Black seizes c4 with his knight. (Lipnitsky – Smyslov,
Moscow 1951)

(389)** Double attack, mate
Both sides have deadly threats, but White strikes first with
1.g4+! Kh4 [1...Kg5 2.Bf4+ snags the rook] **2.Bg3+ Kg5**
[2...Kh3 3.g5 mate] **3.Bf4+** winning material.

(390)* Fork
1.Nb3 Qb6 [or 1...Qb4 2.a3 Qb6 3.Na4] **2.Na4** wins a piece.

391. White to move

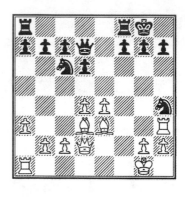

394. Black to move

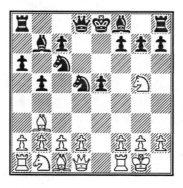

392. White to move

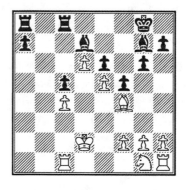

395. White to move

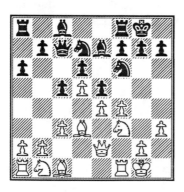

393. Black to move

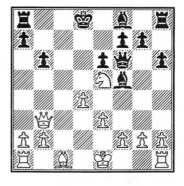

396. White to move

(391)*** Skewer, mating net

White can win a rook or force mate by **1.Re4+! Kf5** [1...Kh5 2.Rh4 mate] **2.Rf4+ Ke5 3.Ra5+ Ke6 4.Rxg5.** White can still stop the passed pawn. Note that 1.f3+! also wins: 1...Rxf3 [1...Kf5 2.Rac6 threatening R2e5 mate 2...Rc5 3.g4+ Kf4 4.R6e4 mate; 1...Kh5 2.g4+ Kh4 3.Rh6+ Rh5 4.Rxh5 mate] 2.Re4+ Kf5 3.Kxf3.

(392)*** Overworked piece

White takes charge by **1.Qh5!** [1.Qf3 is less effective: 1...Qxg5 2.Bxd5 Qg6 and now c6 and f7 are secure; 1.Nxf7!? Kxf7 2.Qf3+ Ke6 is speculative] **1...Qd7.** The Black queen cannot adequately guard both f7 and d5 [1...g6 2.Qf3 Qxg5 3.Bxd5 Kd7 (to defend c6) 4.Qxf7+ wins]. **2.Qxf7+ Qxf7 3.Nxf7 Kxf7 4.Bxd5+** and White is up a clear pawn.

(393)* Fork

1...Nh5 creates the double threat of winning the f4 pawn or going to g3 with a fork.

(394)* Fork

Black wins the exchange by **1...Qxh3! 2.gxh3 Nf3+.**

(395)**** Restrict opponent's piece

1.h4! h6 2.Nh3!!. This stops ...g6-g5, and thus ensures that Black's dark-squared bishop will be imprisoned behind a wall of pawns. [2.Nf3 is less effective due to 2...Bc6.] (Karpov – Kasparov, London 1986)

(396)** Fork, mating net

1.Qb5! threatens mate at d7 [1.Qa4 works just as well]. There is no satisfactory defense: **1...Kc8** [1...Qe7 2.Nc6+ winning the queen] **2.Qd7+ Kb8 3.Nc6** mate.

397. White to move

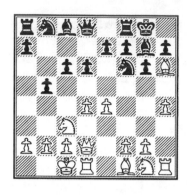

400. Black to move

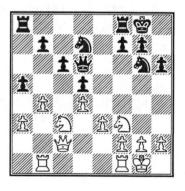

398. Black to move

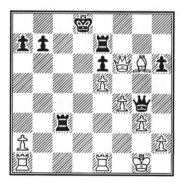

401. Black to move

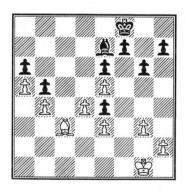

399. White to move

402. White to move

(397)* Trapped piece
1.Ba3 wins the exchange.

(398)*** Turn back minority attack
Black can halt White's intended queenside minority attack by
1...b5! 2.Qb3 Nb6 3.Rfc1 axb4 4.axb4 Nc4. The knight on c4
shields the c6 pawn from attack, and if the knight is exchanged,
Black gets a protected passed pawn.

(399)** Prevent invasion
White is busted if the Black king manages to get to c4. The
White monarch must rush to b3 to stop this. **1.Kf2** [or 1.Kf1]
1...Ke8 2.Ke2 Kd7 3.Kd2 Kc6 4.Kc2 Kd5 5.Kb3 and White
survives to continue the fight.

(400)* Fork, remove the guard
1...b4! safely wins material, for example **2.Nce2** [2.Bxg7 bxc3!
(White is still attacking after 2...Kxg7?! 3.Nb1 Nxe4 4.Qe3 Nf6
5.h5!) 3.Qh6 cxb2+ 4.Kxb2 Ng4 nets a piece] **2...Nxe4 3.Qf4
Bxh6 4.Qxh6 Nxf2**.

(401)** Take the perp
Black has nothing better than to force perpetual check by
1...Rxg3+ 2.hxg3 Qxg3+ 3.Kf1 Qf3+ etc.

(402)*** Salvage bleak endgame
1.Nf1! Ra1 (on other moves the White king just heads toward
c2) **2.Nd2! Rxb1** [2...Bxd2 3.Rxb2 and Black cannot force mate]
3.Nxb1. The pawn is blockaded.

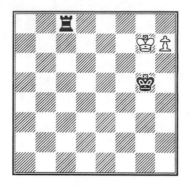

403. Black to move

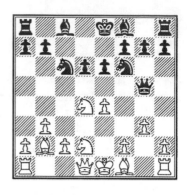

406. White to move

404. White to move

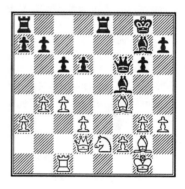

407. Black to move

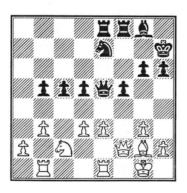

405. White to move

408. White to move

(403)*** Underpromotion, *zugzwang*

1...Rc7+ 2.Kg8 [2.Kh8 Kg6 3.Kg8 Rc8 mate] **2...Kg6** and Black had to be ready for the underpromotion **3.h8N+!?** [3.h8Q Rc8 mate] **3...Kf6 4.Ng6 Kxg6**.

(404)*** Beware the discovered attack

The bishop on g5 is a little loose, putting White in danger of ...Nxe4 tricks. For example, one move to avoid is the otherwise desirable **1.0–0–0?** which loses a pawn to **1...Nxe4! 2.Bxe7** [or 2.Nxe4 Bxe4 3.Bxe7 (3.Qxe4 Bxg5+) 3...Bxf3 4.Bxd8 Bxe2 5.Bxe2 Rxd8] **2...Nxc3 3.Bxd8 Nxe2+** (with White having castled long, this capture comes with check, so the d8 bishop has no chance to escape) **4.Bxe2 Rxd8**. Thus in the game White played **1.Bxf6!** and castled on his next turn. (Rogers – Milos, Manila 1992)

(405)*** Positional pawn play

1.d4! cxd4 [or 1...Qd6 2.dxc5 Qxc5] **2.Nxd4**. White has the better bishop, and the d4 outpost for her knight. She may create a passed pawn by a2-a4. On the other hand, Black's isolated d-pawn is vulnerable on a semi-open file. And with b5 under attack, White will be the first to slide a rook to the open c-file. (Analysis from Nudelman – Justo, Malta 1980)

(406)**** Exposed queen and weak square

White can punish Black's premature queen sortie by **1.Nb5!** (threatening Nc7+, and taking aim at the juicy d6 square) **1...Rb8 2.e5** (hitting d6 again, while clearing e4 for the other knight) **2...Nd7** [2...dxe5 3.Nc7+ Ke7 4.Ba3+ Kd8 5.Ne4+ winning the queen; 2...Nxe5 3.f4 snaring a piece] **3.Ne4** (taking a shot at the Black queen, thus triple-teaming on d6 with gain in time) **3...Qd8 4.exd6** with an overwhelming advantage.

(407)* Double attack, remove the guard

1...Qb2!. Black will win either the pawn on a3 or the one on d3.

(408)* Your pawn or your life

1.Bxc6! picks up a pawn, since **1...bxc6??** loses to **2.Qa6** mate.

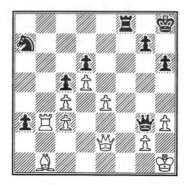

409. Black to move

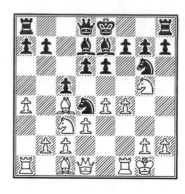

412. White to move

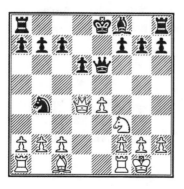

410. Black to move

413. Black to move

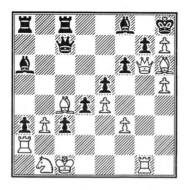

411. White to move

414. White to move

(409)*** Deflection, mate
1...Rf2? would allow 2.Rb8+ Kh7 3.e5+ g6 4.Rb7+ when Black had better accept the perpetual check. **1...a2!!** eliminates this drawing resource by deflecting the bishop from its control of h7. Now **2.Bxa2 Rf2** wins for Black.

(410)* Not so fast – the fork fails!
The hasty fork 1...Nxc2?? loses to 2.Qa4+!. The simple retreat **1...Nc6** is better.

(411)** Interference, mate
1.Bf7! blocks the Black queen's defense of g7, enabling a quick finish: **1...c2** [1...Qxf7 only delays the inevitable] **2.Bxg7+ Bxg7 3.Qxg7** mate.

(412)** Fork, discovered check
1.Nxf7! Kxf7 2.f5!. White regains the piece with a superior position.

(413)*** Sac rook to get passed pawns
Black wins by **1...cxb4!!** sacrificing a rook to create unstoppable passed pawns. **2.Rxc8** [2.axb4 Rxc2 3.Rxc2 a3 4.Ra2 Kd4 is no better] **2...Rxc8 3.Rxc8 bxa3 4.Rc1 b4 5.Ra1 b3**.

(414)*** Restrict enemy forces
After **1.g5! Bc8 2.g4!** the Black pieces have nowhere to go, and nothing to do. (Hort – Ciocâltea, Budapest 1973)

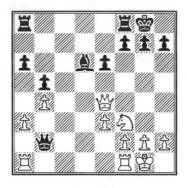

415. White to move

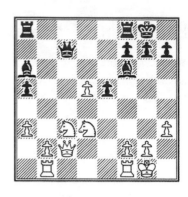

418. Black to move

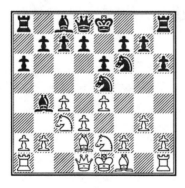

416. White to move

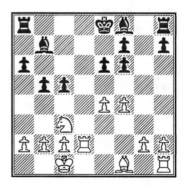

419. White to move

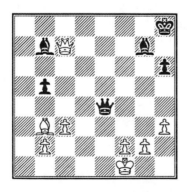

417. White to move

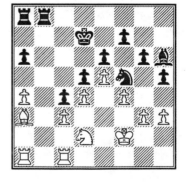

420. Black to move

(415)*** Double attack, fork
White comes up a pawn ahead after **1.Ng5 g6 2.Nxe6! Rfc8** [2...fxe6?? 3.Qxe6+ Kh8 4.Qxd6] **3.Qd4! Be5** [or 3...Qxd4 4.Nxd4] **4.Qxb2 Bxb2 5.Nc7.**

(416)* Parry two threats
White must cope with the threats of ...Nxd3 mate and ...Nf3 mate. **1.Nd4** or **1.Nf4** is best.

(417)*** Attack, safety net, skewer
1.Qb8+ [1.Qd8+? is at best a perpetual check] **1...Kh7 2.Bg8+ Kg6** [2...Kh8 3.Bf7+ with mate to follow] **3.Qg3+ Kf6** [3...Kf5 4.Bh7+; 3...Kh5 4.Bf7+] **4.Qd6+ Kg5 5.h4+!** [White's "safety net" at move 1 was to take the perpetual check here by 5.Qg3+ Kf6 6.Qd6+ etc.] **5...Qxh4** [5...Kxh4 6.Qg3+ Kh5 7.Bf7+; 5...Kg4 6.f3+; 5...Kh5 6.Bf7+ Kg4 7.Qg3+ Kf5 8.Bg6+] **6.Qe7+.** White picks up a bishop, and remains two pawns up.

(418)* Two pins
1...c4! wins material, as both White knights are pinned.

(419)** Double attack, discovered check
1.Nxb5! wins a pawn, the tactical point being **1...axb5?? 2.Bxb5+ Ke7 3.Rd7+** with yet more gains.

(420)** Attack pawn chain
1...h4! wins a pawn: **2.g4** [2.gxh4? Bxf4 3.Rc2 Nxh4 is worse for White] **2...Bxf4 3.gxf5 Bxd2 4.Rc2 Bh6.**

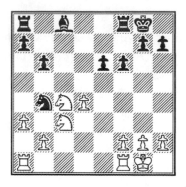

421. Black to move

424. Black to move

422. White to move

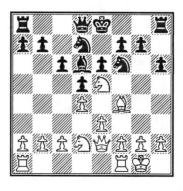

425. White to move

423. Black to move

426. White to move

(421)*** Fork, pin, double attack
Black wins at least a pawn by **1...Nc2! 2.Rad1 Ba6 3.b3 Rfc8 4.Rd2** [4.Ne4 Bxc4 5.bxc4 Rxc4] **4...Nxa3**.

(422)**** Double attack
Here's the way to take advantage of the loose knight on g4. **1.Rdc1 Qb4 2.Rab1 Qd6 3.Rxb8+ Qxb8 4.Bb5+ Kf8** [4...Kd8 5.Qd1+ Bd6 (5...Qd6 6.Qc2) 6.Rc6 Ke7 7.Nh4 followed by Nf5+ or Qxg4] **5.Bd7** with the dual threat of Bxg4 and Rc8+.

(423)* Caught in the net
1...Kc7! wins, as White cannot prevent ...Rd5 mate.

(424)* Discovered attack, overworked piece, pin
1...Nxe4 nets a pawn: **2.Qxe4** [2.Nxe4 Bxa1] **2...Bxc3**.

(425)* Fork, discovered attack
1.Nxf7! [1.Nxc6 also nets a pawn; 1.Ng6? Bxf4 2.Nxh8 Bc7 is no good, as the knight is trapped] **1...Kxf7 2.Bxd6**. White has won a pawn and prevented Black from castling.

(426)** Win a queen, lose the game
1.hxg3. White must capture the knight, restoring material equality. Taking the discovered check would be disastrous, e.g., 1.Nc5+?? Kh8! 2.hxg3 [certainly not 2.Nxb7?? Rf1 mate] 2...dxc5 when White is just a piece down.

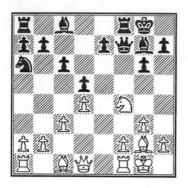

427. White to move

430. White to move

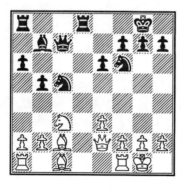

428. Black to move

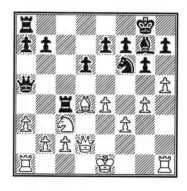

431. Black to move

429. White to move

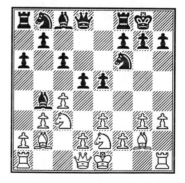

432. Black to move

(427)** Discourage enemy break

Black's plan is to achieve the ...e7-e5 break. White can best resist this by **1.Nd3** followed by [1.Re1 is less attractive due to the latent pressure on f2] **2.Bf4.** (Ivanchuk – Pomes, Terrassa 1991)

(428)** Force back enemy piece

1...b4! forces the c3 knight to retreat to b1 or d1, severely hampering White's development. Worse is **2.Na4?? Qc6** when Black wins a piece.

(429)**** Mating net, skewer

The obvious try 1.Nxd6 Rxd6 2.Qxa7 Rd7 is not a clear win. White can seal the victory, however, with **1.Qe5!** voluntarily unpinning the enemy rook to create a mating threat [1.Qg5+ Kf7 2.Qf4+ Ke7 3.Qe5 comes to the same thing]: **1...Rd5** [1...Kf7 2.Nxd6+; 1...R8d7 2.Nxd6 Rxd6 3.Qxg7+ Ke8 4.Qxb7] **2.Qxg7+ Ke8 3.Nf6** mate.

(430)*** Trapped piece, fork, discovery, exposed king

1.Bc1!! Qxa1 [the threat is 2.Bb2 Qb4 3.a3 Qb5 4.a4 Qb4 5.c3 trapping the Black queen; there is no escape: 1...Qd4 loses to 2.Bb2 Qd7 3.Nb6+; 1...Qb4 is met by 2.Bd2 Qb5 3.a4] **2.Bf4!.** White threatens Nb6 mate, so the Black queen falls. As an alternative, 1.Bd2! Qd4 2.Ba5 wins at least the exchange. The rook cannot hide: 2...Re8 3.c3 Qd7 4.Nb6+.

(431)* Discovered attack

1...Nxc4! wins a pawn: **2.Nxc4** [2.fxe4 Bxd4 and Black picks off yet more material at c3] **2...Qxd2+ 3.Nxd2 Rxd4.**

(432)** Cramp opponent's position

1...d4! 2.Nb1 [or 2.exd4 exd4 3.Nb1 d3] **2...d3.** The pawn on d3 will be a thorn in White's flesh for a long time.

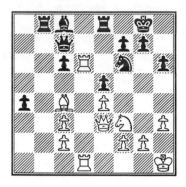

433. White to move

436. White to move

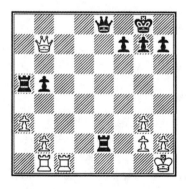

434. Black to move

437. Black to move

435. White to move

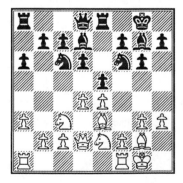

438. Black to move

(433)**** Exchange sac launches offensive
1.Rxf6! gxf6 2.Qxh6 gives White a winning attack. **2...Qe7**
[2...Be6 3.Nh4! and now Black cannot stop both Nf5 and Rd3-
g3(+), e.g., 3...Rbd8 4.Bd5!!; 2...f5 3.Ng5 Be6 4.Qh7+ Kf8
5.Nxe6+ Rxe6 6.Bxe6 fxe4 7.Rd7] **3.Qg6+ Kf8 4.Qh7 Qb7**
5.Nh4 Be6 6.Qh8+ Ke7 7.Ng6+ fxg6 8.Qg7+ Bf7 9.Qxf7 mate.

(434)** Fortify back rank
1...Ra8 is the only move. 1...Rd2? fails to 2.Rc8 Rd8 3.Rbc1!;
similarly 1...Qf8? 2.Rc8 Re8 3.Rbc1!

(435)** Decoy, fork
1.Rb7! ends all resistance: **1...Qxb7 2.Nd6+** wins the queen.
1.Nxd7 Qxd7 2.Nxd6+ Kf8 3.Qxd7 Rxd7 4.Rb8+ nets the
exchange, and should also win.

(436)* Double attack
1.Qd4+ picks off the loose rook on a7.

(437)** Deflection, mate
1...f4! creates the threat of mate by Rh1. White must reply
2.Rxf4 allowing **2...Rh1+** [the immediate 2...Rxc3? admits too
much counterplay: 3.Rf7+ Kc8 4.Rxa7 Rxc5 5.Rf2! Kb8 6.Rxh7
etc.] **3.Kg3 Rxc3+** winning the knight.

(438)*** Consistency, central structure, time
1...exd4 is called for. This justifies the placement of the rook on
e8, which now pressures the c4 pawn. On other moves, White
can close the center by d4-d5; Black would then have wasted one
tempo on ...Rf8-e8, and must waste another to move it back (in
support of the...f7-f5 break).

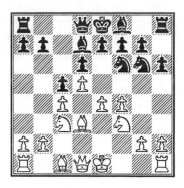

439. White to move

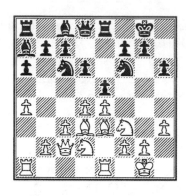

442. Black to move

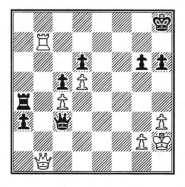

440. White to move

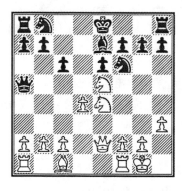

443. White to move

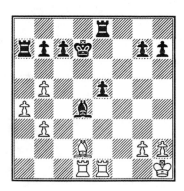

441. White to move

444. Black to move

(439)*** Pawn storm, mate

It's hard to argue against 1.0–0 or 1.Qc2, but already after **1.e5!**, Black must cough up a piece or be mated: **1...Ng8** [1...dxe5 2.fxe5 amounts to the same thing: 2...Ng8 3.e6 Bc8 4.exf7+ Kxf7 5.Bxg6+ Kxg6 6.Nh4+ Kf6 7.Qf3+ Bf5 8.Qxf5 mate] **2.e6 Bc8** [2...fxe6 3.Bxg6 mate] **3.exf7+ Kxf7 4.Bxg6+ Kxg6 5.Nh4+ Kf6 6.Ne4+ Kf7 7.Qh5+ g6 8.Qxg6** mate.

(440)*** Prevent perpetual check

White would like to capture at g6, creating mating threats, but Black might get a perpetual check starting with Qe5+. Thus **1.Re7!** first. Now Black must give up his queen or be mated: **1...Ra8 2.Qxg6.**

(441)*** Pins

White wins at least two pawns by **1.Bf4! c5** [not 1...exf4? 2.Rxd4+ Kc8 3.Rxe8 mate] **2.bxc6+ bxc6 3.Rxe5 c5** [or 3...Rxe5 4.Bxe5 c5 5.Bxd4 cxd4 6.Rxd4+] **4.Rxc5 Re1+ 5.Rxe1 Bxc5.**

(442)*** Dissolve enemy pawn center

This is just the right moment for **1...exd4! 2.Nxd4** [2.cxd4 would allow 2...Nb4] **2...Ne5 3.Bf1 d5!.** By dissolving White's pawn center, Black has equalized. (Tarrasch – Alekhine, Baden-Baden 1925)

(443)** Piece for 3 pawns and more

1.Nxf7!. White gets at least three pawns and the initiative for a knight: **1...Kxf7 2.Ng5+ Ke8 3.Qxe6 Rf8 4.Qc8+ Qd8 5.Qxb7 Nbd7**. White has the pleasant choice between 6.Qxc6, 6.Ne6 or 6.Re1.

(444)* Overworked piece

1...Ne2+ 2.Kh1 Nxc1 3.Rxc1 Bxf2 leaves Black a pawn up.

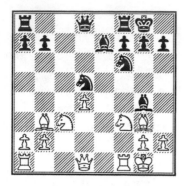

445. Black to move

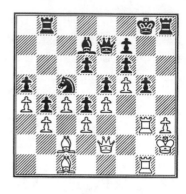

448. White to move

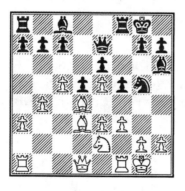

446. White to move

449. White to move

447. White to move

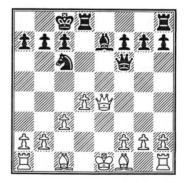

450. Black to move

(445)* Fork
1...Ne3 wins the exchange.

(446)**** Restrict enemy piece
1.c6! (threatening Bc5 winning the exchange) **1...b6** [on 1...Rd8 White just keeps up the pressure, e.g., 2.Rc1 a6 3.Qa4] **2.b5 a6 3.a4**. Remarkably, Black's light-squared bishop has become imprisoned. White can conduct kingside operations effectively a piece up. (Petrosian – Fischer, Bled 1959)

(447)* Pin
1.Qe6+ Kh7 [or 1...Kh8 2.Rh6+] **2.Rf7** wins the queen.

(448)*** Rook sac, discovered check
White wins material by **1.Rxg5+! fxg5** [1...Kf8 2.Qh5! wins a rook due to 2...Rxh5 3.Rg8 mate] **2.Bxg5 Kf8** [there is no escape: 2...Qe8 3.Be7+ Kh7 4.Qh5 mate] **3.Bxe7+ Kxe7**.

(449)** Overworked piece, double check
White can win back a pawn by **1.Nxd6!**. Indeed, if the knight is captured, then White nets a second pawn: **1...Qxd6 2.Qxg7+ Kxg7 3.Bxe5+**.

(450)** Pin, double attack
Black should snatch back a pawn by **1...Nxd4!**. If the knight is taken, then White loses his queen: **2.cxd4? Bb4+ 3.Bd2** [3.Kd1 Rxd4+] **3...Rhe8**.

162

451. Black to move

454. White to move

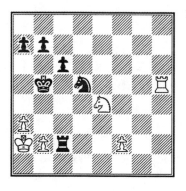

452. White to move

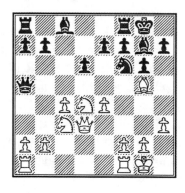

455. White to move

453. White to move

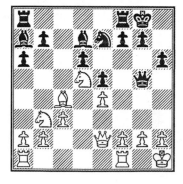

456. Black to move

(451)** Trapped piece, remove the guard
Black wins a piece by **1...Ke6 2.Rxf7 Rh8 3.Bg6 Rh6 4.Rg7 Kf6**.

(452)** Trapped piece, fork
1.Kb1! wins the exchange – there is no safe square for the rook. **1...Rc4** [1...Re2 2.Nc3+] **2.Nd6+**.

(453)** Obstruct enemy development
1.Qb4 momentarily stops Black from castling. There followed **1...Nd5 2.Qa3 Qe7 3.Bb5+ Bd7 4.Bxd7+** and Black still cannot castle short after either recapture. (Topalov – Bareev, Dortmund 2002)

(454)** Deflection
1.Rf1+ Kc2 2.Rf2+! deflects the Black rook from coverage of the passed pawn.

(455)** Create target and outpost
1.Bxf6! exf6 [or 1...Bxf6 2.Nd5 Bd7 3.Nxf6+ exf6] **2.Nd5**. White's knights are well placed and the d6 pawn will be a target.

(456)**** Disregard enemy outpost!
Black's first impulse might be to swap off the knight on d5. However, after any exchanges at d5, White is left with a dangerously posted piece. For example, after 1...Nxd5 2.Bxd5 Bc6 3.Rad1 Bxd5 4.Rxd5 the backward d6 pawn is in for serious pain. Instead, Black might reason that the d5 knight is not accomplishing much by itself; in fact, it is hindering the bishop on c4 and blocking the d6 pawn from immediate danger. Therefore, Black ought to pursue his own plans before White can develop serious threats. In the game his choice was **1...Ng6!!**, preserving the knight, with ideas about an eventual ...Nf4 and ...f7-f5. (Berelovich – Svidler, Moscow 2003)

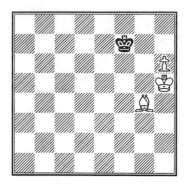

457. White to move

460. White to move

458. Black to move

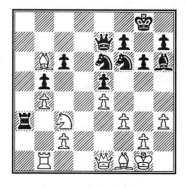

461. Black to move

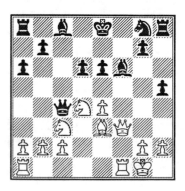

459. White to move

462. White to move

(457)** Wrong-colored bishop

If the Black king could get to g8 or h8 this would be a draw, as the bishop doesn't control the promotion square. The only way to secure the full point is **1.Be6+! Kf8** [1...Kxe6 2.h7; 1...Kf6 2.Bg8] **2.Kg6** and the pawn marches forth.

(458)* Double attack, weak back rank

1...Rd5! wins the knight, due to White's back rank weakness.

(459)*** Pawn sac propels attack

White adds fuel to his attack by **1.e5! dxe5**. The pawn sacrifice has opened the d-file for White's other rook, and cleared e4 for the knight on c3. Black's doubled isolated e-pawns get in the way of his own bishops. There followed **2.Ne4** threatening the fork Nd6+ **2...Qc7 3.Qg3!** defending the d4 knight by pinning e5 **3...Ne7 4.Rad1** seizing the newly opened file. (Nunn – A. Sokolov, Dubai 1986)

(460)**** Liquidate outside pawns

White's queenside pawns are doomed. **1.a5!** ensures that Black's otherwise dangerous a-pawn goes down, too [1.f4? only draws after 1...exf3!; 1.Kf1?? Kc5 2.Kg2 Kb4 3.Kh3 Kxa4 4.Kxh4 Kxb5 and it is Black who wins the foot race]. **1...h3 2.Kf1 Kc5 3.b6 axb6 4.axb6 Kxb6 5.Kg1**.

(461)**** Control of weak squares

1...Nd4! cuts off White's dark-squared bishop from the vulnerable dark squares around his king. **2.Bc5 Qe6 3.Bd3** (defending c2) **3...Nd7 4.Bxd4** [worse is 4.Ne2 Nxc5 5.bxc5 Be3+ 6.Kh1 Nxe2 7.Qxe2 Bxc5] **4...exd4 5.Ne2 Be3+**. White was forced to part with his valuable defender, whereas Black's bishop has become a monster. (Smyslov – Botvinnik, Moscow 1958)

(462)*** Skewer

1.Rg4! wins a pawn: **1...g6 2.Rh4 h5 3.g4** and White will capture twice on h5, since **3...hxg4?** would allow **4.Rh8+**. (Alekhine – Marshall, St. Petersburg 1914)

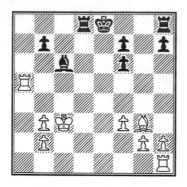

463. White to move

466. White to move

464. White to move

467. White to move

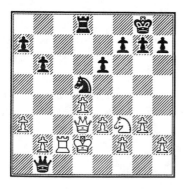

465. White to move

468. White to move

(463)** Indefensible pawn
1.Bh4! picks off the f6 pawn, as **1...Ke7??** [1...Rd6?? is punished by 2.Ra8+] meets with **2.Re5+ Kd6 3.Bxf6** snaring the exchange.

(464)** Trapped piece
1.Qf3 attacks f7 and denies flight squares to the Black queen. After **1...f6 2.Rc1 Qh2 3.Ng4 Qh3 4.Rh1** the queen is trapped.

(465)** Discovered attack
White wins at least a pawn by **1.Ng5! g6** [1...Nf6 2.Nxf7! is similar] **2.Nxf7!** as **2...Kxf7? 3.Rc7+** uncovers an attack on the Black queen.

(466)* Exposed king
1.Rd7!. Black must give up his queen, or else be mated, e.g., **1...Qc8 2.Qe5+ Kg8 3.Rg7+ Kh8 4.Rf7+ Kg8 5.Qg7** mate.

(467)* Double attack
1.e5! wins material, for if **1...Ng8** then **2.Qf3** with a double attack on a8 and f7.

(468)*** Pawn sac creates weaknesses
After the (temporary) pawn sac **1.d5! Rxd5 2.Rxd5 exd5 3.b3**, White has two safe and solid pawn islands, compared to Black's six fully isolated pawns. White will regain a pawn soon, then attack the remaining pawn weaknesses. (Deep Blue – Kasparov, Philadelphia 1996)

469. White to move

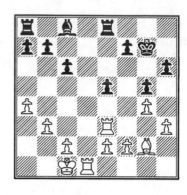

472. Black to move

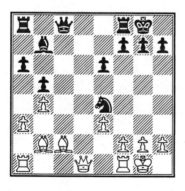

470. White to move

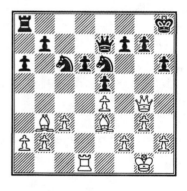

473. White to move

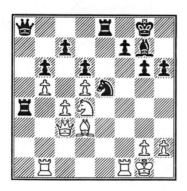

471. Black to move

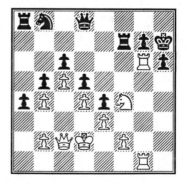

474. White to move

(469)**** Attack, fork
White wins at least the exchange after **1.Nf6+! Kh8** [1...gxf6 2.Bxe6 Qe3 (2...fxe6 3.Qg6+ Kh8 4.Rd7 with mate to follow) 3.Qg6+ Kh8 4.Qxf6+ Kg8 5.Rd7 winning] **2.Bxe6! Qc7** [2...fxe6 3.Nd7; 2...Qc6 3.Nd7; 2...gxf6 3.Qxh6+ Kg8 4.Bf5 mate to follow] **3.Nd7 Qxe6 4.Nxf8 Rxf8**.

(470)* Double attack
1.Bxe4 Bxe4 2.Qd4 with the double threat of Qxe4 and Qxg7 mate.

(471)*** Overworked piece
1...Ra3 2.Rb3 [2.Qc2 Nxd3]. Now the White queen is struggling to defend b3, d3 and d4. **2...Nxd3! 3.Rxa3** [3.Qxd3 Bxd4+] **3...Bxd4+ 4.Qxd4 Qxa3**.

(472)** An ounce of prevention
1...a5 or **1...a6** is necessary to prevent a4-a5-a6 and the resulting tactical problems down the long diagonal. (Polugaevsky – Tal, Leningrad 1971)

(473)*** Assail backward pawn
1.Bb6! prevents the Black rook from coming to the aid of the backward d-pawn. **1...Nb8** (intending ...Nd7 to expel the bishop; otherwise White plays Rd2 and Qd1) **2.Bxe6 fxe6 3.Qh4!** (to remove the only defender of d6) **3...Qd7 4.Qd8+ Qxd8 5.Bxd8** and the embattled pawn is lost. (Smyslov – Reshevsky, Moscow 1948)

(474)*** Fork
White wins by **1.Rxg7+! Rxg7 2.Rxg7+ Kh8** [2...Kxg7 allows 3.Ne6+ snaring the queen] **3.Qd1!** with a winning attack.

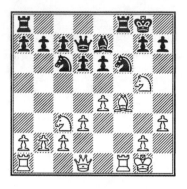

475. Black to move

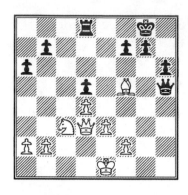

478. Black to move

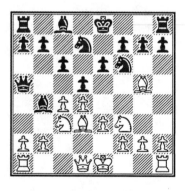

476. White to move

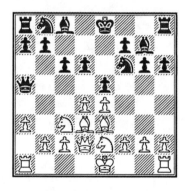

479. Black to move

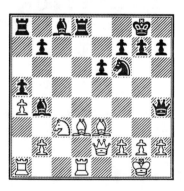

477. White to move

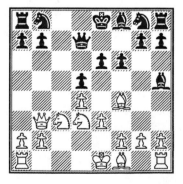

480. White to move

(475)* Discovered attack
1...h6 2.Nf3 Nxe4 nets a pawn because of the loose bishop on f4.

(476)*** The pawn is lost anyway
Black threatens to win a pawn by capturing twice on c3. White's best course would be to accept the loss of the pawn in return for a sizeable lead in development: **1.0–0!** [reinforcing c3 is futile anyway, e.g., 1.Rc1 dxc4 2.Bxc4 Ne4 with attacks on c3 and g5] **1...Bxc3 2.bxc3 Qxc3 3.Rc1 Qa5 4.Qc2 0–0 5.Bf4**. White stands well; Black has difficulty getting his bishop into play.

(477)** Deflection, discovered attack
1.g3! Qh3 2.Bxh7+ Kxh7 3.Rxd8 picks up the exchange and a pawn. The immediate 1.Bxh7?? doesn't quite work, as d8 is protected after 1...Nxh7.

(478)* Trapped piece
1...g6 traps the bishop.

(479)* Grab the bishop pair
Black should snap off White's dark squared bishop by **1...Ng4**. This not only lowers the heat on h6 (enabling Black to castle short), but also enhances the strength of Black's fianchettoed bishop. After any other move, such as 1...Nbd7, White could play 2.f3 preventing this exchange.

(480)** Clearance, pin
1.Bxb8! Rxb8 2.Nf4 wins the bishop on h5 due to the additional threat of Bb5, pinning and winning the queen.

481. White to move

484. Black to move

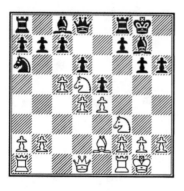

482. Black to move

485. Black to move

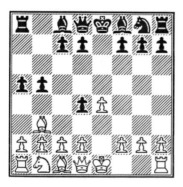

483. White to move

486. White to move

(481)*** Prevent exchange sac
Black would get a winning attack out of 1...Rxf3! 2.gxf3 Nxe5 3.Nd4 Nf4. **1.Ned4** is an effective antidote.

(482)*** Destroy enemy pawn center
1...c6! 2.Bxa6 [2.Nc3 exd4 3.Nxd4 Nxc5] **2...cxd5 3.Bd3 exd4 4.cxd6 dxe4 5.Bxe4 Qxd6**. Black has won a pawn.

(483)** Double attack
White wins the exposed rook on a8 as follows: **1.Bxf7+!** [not 1.Qf3? Qf6] **1...Kxf7** [1...Ke7 2.Bxg8 Rxg8 3.Qh5 is miserable for Black] **2.Qh5+ g6** [other replies are similarly handled, e.g., 2...Ke7 3.Qe5+ Kf7 4.Qd5+] **3.Qd5+**.

(484)** Nearly trapped piece
The White knight at g5 doesn't have many safe squares. Now **1...Qd6!** takes away e6. The threat is ...h7-h6, trapping the knight. White must therefore choose between 2.Qe2, 2.Ne5, or 2.c4, in each case surrendering a pawn to rescue the piece.

(485)** King position, fix weakness
1...Bb1 [1...a5 is less effective, as after 2.e4 the White queenside is out of immediate danger] **2.a3 a5**. Black has cemented the weakness of b3, and cleared the way for his king to advance. (Smyslov – Keres, Moscow 1952)

(486)*** Exchange sac
White is up a pawn, but it is difficult to make headway while Black maintains his well posted knight. However, White creates winning chances by **1.Rc7+! Nxc7 2.Rxc7+ Kd8 3.Rxf7!**, for example **3...Rxa3 4.f5 exf5 5.e6 Re8 6.d5**.

487. Black to move

490. White to move

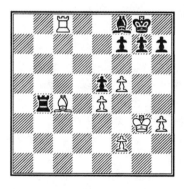

488. White to move

491. White to move

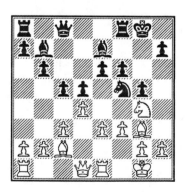

489. Black to move

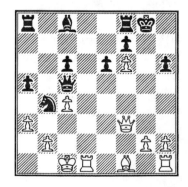

492. White to move

(487)** Attack second weakness

With c4 already under siege, Black strains White's defenses by going after the weak a-pawn: **1...Rh1 2.Kd2** [2.Kc2 Ra1 3.Kb3 Re1] **2...Ra1 3.Bd1 Bxc4**.

(488)*** Keep enemy piece pinned

1.f4! kicks off the winning idea of sending a pawn down the e-file. (1.Rc7 Bd6 2.Bxf7+? would win a pawn, but at the cost of freeing the enemy bishop. Following 2...Kf8 3.Rd7 Be7 4.Bd5 Black can hope to draw by blockading the extra White pawn.) After **1...exf4+ 2.Kxf4 Rb7 3.e5 Re7** Black is nearly in *zugzwang* – eventually his rook will have to desert the e-file. The finish was **4.h4 h6 5.h5 Ra7 6.e6 g5+ 7.hxg6 Kg7 8.gxf7 Bd6+ 9.Ke4 h5 10.Rg8+ Kh6 11.f6**.

(489)* Head 'em off at the pass

1...h5! wins a piece since both the knight and bishop need to escape via f2: **2.Nf2** [2.Bxf5 is no better: 2...exf5 3.Nh6+ Kg7] **2...h4**.

(490)** Stop two threats

Black is threatening not only ...Rxb2, but also ...Nf4, attacking the guard for the c6 knight. **1.Bc1** is the only way to meet both threats.

(491)*** Strain the defender

1.Nd5! strains Black's defense of h7. **1...Qd6** [the knight cannot be captured: 1...cxd5?? 2.Qxc7; 1...Nxd5?? 2.Bxh7+ Nxh7 (2...Kh8 3.Nxf7 mate) 3.Qxh7+ Kf8 4.Qh8 mate] **2.Nxf6+ Qxf6 3.Bxh7+ Kh8 4.Bd3** and White has won a critical pawn.

(492)** Interference

1.Rd5!! wins on the spot. The rook interferes with the Black queen's defense against Qg4+, followed by mate at g7. Black must either give up his queen or succumb to the mate.

493. Black to move

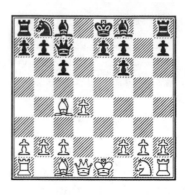

496. White to move

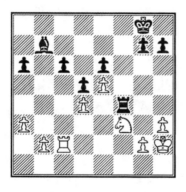

494. White to move

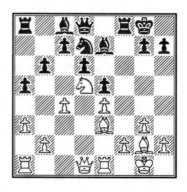

497. White to move

495. White to move

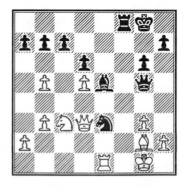

498. Black to move

(493) Trapped piece**
Black wins a piece by **1...g6 2.Bh3 g5 3.Nfe2 g4**.

(494)* Fork, mate, trapped piece**
1.Ng5! wins the pawn on e6. Indeed, if **1...Rxd4?** [1...Bc8?
2.Rxc6 Bd7 3.Rxa6 (threatening Ra8+ with mate to follow)
3...h6 4.Nf3 and White has picked up two pawns.] then **2.Nxc6
Rc4** [2...Re4 3.Nc5 wins the bishop] **3.Rf2** (threatening Rf8
mate) **3...h6 4.Rf8+ Kh7 5.Rb8** and the bishop is trapped.

(495)* Improve piece, attack weaknesses**
1.Nd2!. The knight is heading for c4 where it will attack weak
Black pawns. Note that White is undeterred by **1...Bh6 2.Nc4!
Bxc1 3.Bxd6 Qd8 4.Bxf8**.

(496) Restrict enemy piece**
White should play **1.Qh5!**. The threat to f7 forces **1...e6** after
which Black's light-squared bishop is bad indeed. After 1...e5 the
bishop still has nowhere to go! (Jamieson – Tal, Nice 1974)

(497)* Double attack
1.Nxe7+ Qxe7 2.Qd5+ wins the rook on a8.

(498) Remove the guard, deflection**
1...Nxg2 2.Kxg2 Bxc3 3.Qxc3 Qxd5+ wins a pawn.

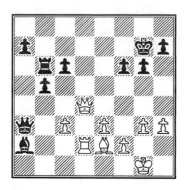

499. White to move

502. White to move

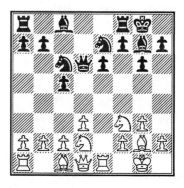

500. Black to move

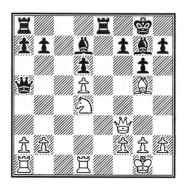

503. Black to move

501. White to move

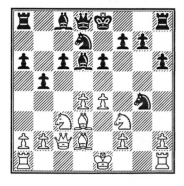

504. White to move

(499)**** Clearance, interference, attack
Black has snatched a pawn at a2, leaving his king vulnerable. The immediate 1.Qd7+ is adequately handled by 1...Bf7. White wins by **1.c4!** interfering with the Black bishop's return to defense. **1...Bxc4** [1...Rb7?? drops the bishop to 2.Qa1] **2.Bxc4 bxc4 3.Qd7+** with a winning attack.

(500)*** Respond to threat
White's threat is 1.Ne4! winning at least a pawn: 2...Qd5 (to protect c5) 3.Nfg5 (now the Black queen must move again, due to the threat of Nf6+) 3...Qd8 [3...Qf5 4.Nxh7! Kxh7 5.g4! wins the Black queen; similarly 3...Qe5 4.Nxh7!] 4.Nxc5. Defending the pawn by **1...b6** is sufficient to maintain the balance; **1...Qc7** has also been played here.

(501)** The scramble
With the Black king cut off along a file, and with the pawn sufficiently advanced, the White king can force its way in front of the pawn: **1.Kc5 Rc8+ 2.Kb6 Rd8 3.Kc6 Rc8+ 4.Kd7**. Now it is a matter of reaching the Lucena position, which is a book win.

(502)*** Don't snatch the pawn!
Black cannot save his d-pawn after 1.Be6?, but he wouldn't need to: 1...c3 2.bxc3 [or 2.Bxd5 Bd3+! 3.Kxd3 cxb2 and Black will promote] 2...b2 3.Bxd5 Bd3+ 4.Kxd3 b1Q+. Instead, **1.Kd2** or **1.Kd1** maintains the status quo.

(503)* Back rank weakness
1...Bxd4 simply wins a piece, as **2.Rxd4??** allows a back rank mate.

(504)* Trapped piece, fork
1.e5! wins a piece, for if the bishop retreats, then **2.h3** traps the knight (the moves may be reversed).

505. White to move

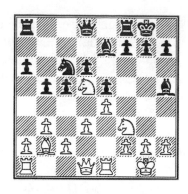

508. White to move

506. White to move

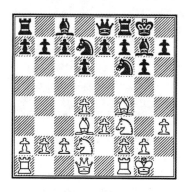

509. Black to move

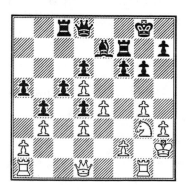

507. Black to move

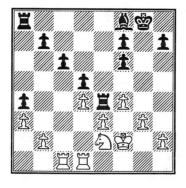

510. White to move

(505)** Discovered attack, control important square
After **1.Ne4! Qc7** [1...Nxe4 2.Qxc6 Rb8 3.Bxe4 White has won a pawn] **2.Nxd6+ Qxd6 3.e4 Qc7 4.b4**, White enjoys the bishop pair, and his grip on c5 stifles counterplay.

(506)**** Patience!
White has the edge in this position, due to the harmonious placement of his rooks, the somewhat exposed condition of the Black king, and the light square weaknesses in Black's pawn formation. These fragile assets would evaporate if queens were exchanged, so White goes for **1.Qd1!!**. The superficially appealing centralization 1.Qd5? merely invites Black to repeat his offer by 1...Qg8. Now 2.Qd1 would allow 2...d5 when Black's central steamroller gets under way. (Adams – Tiviakov, Wijk aan Zee 2003)

(507)** Deny enemy outpost
1...Bf8 is needed here, intending **...Bh6**, to activate the bishop and to prevent Ng3-e2-f4-e6.

(508)*** Because she's worth it
1.Nxe5! Bxd1 [White is a healthy pawn up after 1...dxe5 2.Qxh5] **2.Nxc6 Qd7 3.Ncxe7+ Kh8 4.Raxd1** leaves White with a pawn and three aggressively deployed minor pieces for the queen. The Black heavy pieces have little scope with all the pawns around.

(509)* Fork
1...e5! wins material: **2.dxe5 dxe5 3.Bh2 e4**.

(510)** Struggle for better minor piece
1.g4! discourages Black from trying ...f6-f5 (to limit the White knight and improve the scope of his bishop), and clears the way for Ne2-g3-f5. From f5, the knight will lend support to the e3 pawn, and dominate the opposing bishop.

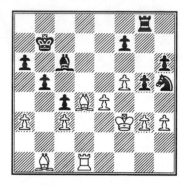

511. White to move

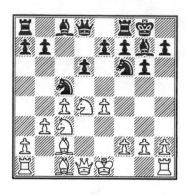

514. Black to move

512. Black to move

515. Black to move

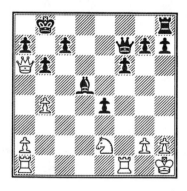

513. White to move

516. Black to move

(511)*** Target weak pawn

White wins by targeting the weak h6 pawn: **1.Kg4 Ng7 2.Bxg7 Rxg7 3.Kh5 Rh7 4.Rd6 Be8!?** (setting a trap) **5.f6** [of course not 5.Rxh6?? f6+ dropping the rook] **5...Rh8 6.e5 Ka7 7.Be4**. Black has no useful moves.

(512)** Stop two plans

White would like to play Re7, with counterplay, or Kg2, freeing his cornered rook. **1...Qh3!** stops both ideas, and wins the f3 pawn as well.

(513)** Prevent double attack

Ahead a rook for three pawns, White was eager to rip open the a-file for a quick finish by 1.a4?? overlooking 1...Bc4 (double attack) 2.b5 Bxe2 3.a5 [3.Rfc1 Bg4 4.a5 Bc8 traps the White queen] 3...Bxf1 4.axb6 Bxg2+ 5.Kxg2 cxb6 winning easily. **1.Rac1** stops the threat and preserves White's winning advantage [1.Nd4 is also good, as 1...Bc4?? 2.Nc6+ leads to mate].

(514)** Double attack

Black nets a pawn by **1...Nfxe4!** since **2.Nxe4** [or 2.Bxe4 Nxe4 3.Nxe4 Qa5+ 4.Qd2 Qe5] **2...Nxe4 3.Bxe4 Qa5+** followed by ...Qe5 regains the piece.

(515)** Fork, trapped piece

1...Bxf2+! [or 1...Qb6 first] wins material: **2.Kxf2 Qb6+ 3.Kg3 Qxb2 4.Nc3 Nxc3 5.dxc3 Qxc3+**.

(516)**** Tactic loses, take the perp

The tactical try 1...Rxb2+? 2.Qxb2 Qh2+ 3.Kf3 Qxb2 wins the White queen, but loses the game due to back rank issues: 4.Bf7! Qa3+ [4...g6 5.h6; 4...h6 5.Re8+ Kh7 6.Bg6 mate] 5.Re3 Qf8 6.Re8 Qxe8 7.Bxe8. Rather, Black should take the perpetual check **1...Qh2+ 2.Kf1** [2.Ke3?? drops the queen to a skewer: 2...Qg3+] **2...Qh1+ 3.Kf2** etc. [after 3.Ke2? Rxb2+ 4.Qxb2 Qg2+ 5.Kd3 Qxb2 Black is winning].

517. Black to move

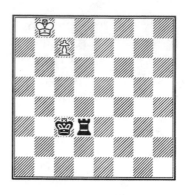

520. Black to move

518. White to move

521. Black to move

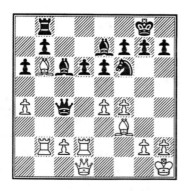

519. White to move

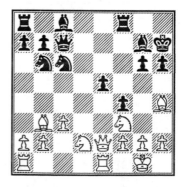

522. Black to move

(517)** Discovered attack, double attack
White loses material after **1...Nxe4 2.Bxe7 Qxe7 3.Qxe4 Qb4+** followed by ...Qxb2.

(518)* Skewer, double attack
White wins the exchange by **1.Bf1 Re5 2.Bf4.**

(519)* Trapped piece
1.Rd4 Qc3 2.Rb3 and the Black queen is trapped.

(520)** Perpetual check, skewer
1...Kb2!! secures a draw: **2.c8Q** [2.Kc8 Rc3] **2...Rb3+** with endless checks along the a- and b-files, or an equalizing skewer.

(521)*** Prevent enemy castling
After **1...Bb4+! 2.axb4 Bxb5 3.bxa5 Bc4 4.Qa3 bxa5** the material situation is level, but Black has prevented her opponent from castling. That was all she needed to launch a successful attack. (Karpov – J. Polgár, Wijk aan Zee 2003)

(522)*** Don't trap the piece
Black can trap a piece momentarily by 1...g5? but it comes to a net loss after **2.Nxg5+!** hxg5 **3.Qh5+** Bh6 **4.Bxg5** Qg7 **5.Bc2+** Bf5 **6.Bxh6** Qxh6 **7.Bxf5+.** Better is **1...Bf5** protecting the delicate b1–h7 diagonal.

523. White to move

526. Black to move

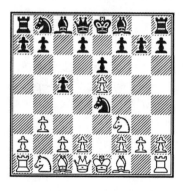

524. White to move

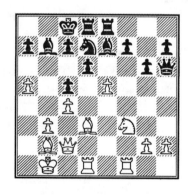

527. White to move

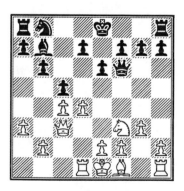

525. Black to move

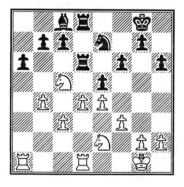

528. White to move

(523)**** Anticipate counterplay

Before committing to the natural lunge 1.Qa7?, White had better take into account 1...Qh4!!. Now 2.Qxc7 [or 2.Bf2 Bxd4!; 2.Kg2 Ra8!] would allow Black tremendous counterplay starting with 2...Qg3+. Instead, **1.Kg2** or **1.Qf2** holds the line.

(524)** Trapped piece, pin

1.d3 Qa5+ 2.c3! Nxc3 3.Qd2 wins a piece.

(525)*** Seize central square

1...Bxf3! 2.Qxf3 [or 2.exf3 Nc6] **2...Qxf3 3.exf3 Nc6**. The Black knight will take residence on d4, from where it cannot be dislodged.

(526)*** Clearance, fork, skewer

Black wins a pawn by **1...Rxg3!! 2.fxg3** [worse is 2.Rxd4 Rxg2 3.Rd2 Rg4] **2...Nb3+ 3.Kc2 Nxd2** since **4.Kxd2?** would drop at least a second pawn to **4...Rxb2+**. (Analysis from Hutchings – Keene, Woolacombe 1973)

(527)*** Remove key defender

White has initiated a queenside pawn storm, but there is not yet a knockout punch. A logical next step is **1.Be4!** to exchange the defender of the weak light squares around the enemy king. (Padevsky – Kholmov, Dresden 1956)

(528)** Close position advantageously

1.d5! closes the center strongly in White's favor: Black's minor pieces have no decent squares; his rooks are doubled against a brick wall, and he has no useful pawn breaks (for example, 1...f5 2.c4 fxe4 3.fxe4 helps White). White, on the other hand, will keep pushing his queenside pawns, well supported by his knights and rooks.

529. White to move

532. White to move

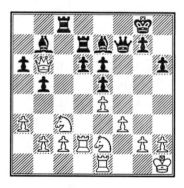

530. Black to move

533. White to move

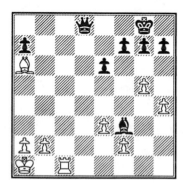

531. Black to move

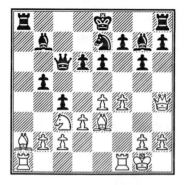

534. Black to move

(529)*** Deny crucial squares
1.Nf5! Ng2 [1...Nxf5 2.Kxf5 and White wins the foot race; 1...Kxb4 2.Nxh4 is similar] **2.Ke5!** preventing the knight from reaching f4 and stopping the pawn. (Timman – Ree, Amsterdam 1984)

(530)** Powerful break
1...d5! opens up the position much to Black's favor. For example, after **2.exd5** [on 2.Qf2 d4 3.Nd1 Bg5 White must give up the exchange or a pawn] **2...exd5** Black enjoys the bishop pair, two strong center pawns, and a grip on the c-file. On the other hand, White's knights lack support points.

(531)* Defense, weak back rank
1...Bc6! defends against the deadly ...Rc8(+), leaving Black with a winning material advantage. The bishop cannot be captured due to White's weak back rank.

(532)** Promotion, discovered check
White has **1.Rc8! Rxa7** (or else the pawn promotes) **2.Kb6+** winning the rook.

(533)*** Pressure weak pawn
1.b3! clears a path for Nd3-b2-c4. **1...g5 2.Kf2 Rb7 3.Nb2 Rb5 4.Nc4** defending the a5 pawn and putting maximum force on the backward d6 pawn. (Anand – Ivanchuk, Monaco 2001)

(534)*** Pin, fork, remove the guard
1...b4! 2.Nd1 [2.Ne2 Nf5! 3.Qf2 (3.exf5?? Qxg2 mate) 3...Nxe3 4.Qxe3 Bxb2 attacking the guard of a2] **2...b3 3.cxb3 cxb3** wins the pinned bishop.

535. Black to move

538. White to move

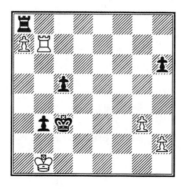

536. Black to move

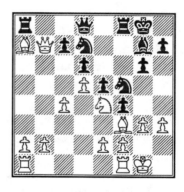

539. Black to move

537. White to move

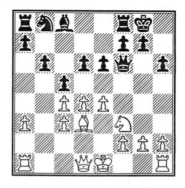

540. White to move

(535)** Extract concession
Against the irritating **1...Bg4!**, White has three options, none pleasant: (1) trade off his precious light-squared bishop; (2) block the bishop (and weaken his kingside) by f2-f3; or (3) lose material.

(536)* Mating threat
1...Re8! [or ...Rf8] **2.Rxb3+ Kxb3 3.Kc1 Ra8** is the easiest win.

(537)*** Obstruct adversary's development
Clearly Black needs to develop his kingside and castle. However, **1.Bd4!** holds the f8 bishop to the defense of the g-pawn. Black now has to play something awkward such as **1...f6** in order to complete his development. This will make the forthcoming g2-g4-g5 all the more effective. (Short – Pogorelov, Gibraltar 2004)

(538)**** Quarterback sweep
White breaks through by **1.g4! fxg4** [or 1...hxg4 2.h5! gxh5 3.Bxf5+ Ke7 4.Rhxh5; 1...Rdf8 2.gxf5+ gxf5 3.Rhg1 Rxg5 4.Rxg5] **2.Bxg6 Rdf8 3.Rf1** and White will mop up the g- and h-pawns, winning. (Analysis from Kasparov – Bacrot, Sarajevo 2000)

(539)** Trapped piece, remove the guard
Black has given up two pawns for an attack on the White king. The attack itself has stalled – there is no breakthrough via g3, for example. Still, Black gets the upper hand by **1...Qc8!** humiliating the bishop on a7.

(540)*** Nearly trapped piece
White can win at least a pawn due to the vulnerable rook on a8. **1.e5!** clearing e4 for the bishop **1...Qd8** [1...Qe7 2.Be4 Bb7 3.exd6 White keeps the extra pawn] **2.dxc5 Bb7** [2...bxc5 3.Be4 d5 4.cxd5 Bb7 5.c4; 2...dxc5 3.Be4] **3.cxd6**.

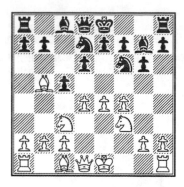

541. White to move

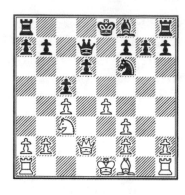

544. White to move

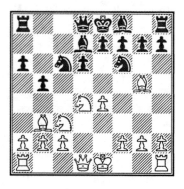

542. White to move

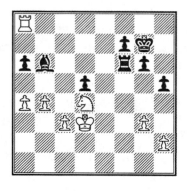

545. White to move

543. White to move

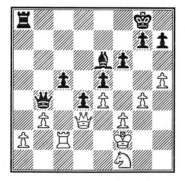

546. Black to move

(541)*** Fork, central advance
1.e5! Ng4 [1...dxe5 2.dxe5 is even worse] **2.e6! fxe6 3.Ng5**
White regains the pawn with a superior position.

(542)*** Target weak squares
Black should have played ...e7-e6 earlier in order to blunt the
bishop on b3. Now f7 is vulnerable and the knight on c6 is a
little shaky. White takes advantage by **1.Bxf6!** (giving his queen
access to h5 and d5) **1...exf6** [1...gxf6 2.Nxc6 Bxc6 3.Qh5 and f7
cannot be defended any further] **2.Qh5 Qe7** [2...g6 3.Bxf7+
Kxf7 4.Qd5+ Kg7 5.Nxc6] **3.0-0-0.** White enjoys an enormous
advantage.

(543)** Outside passed pawn
1.Rxh5+! Rxh5 2.Bxh5 Kxh5 3.b5. A White pawn will
promote.

(544)** Stop enemy castling
1.h4! prevents Black from castling long (due to Bh3), allows the
White bishop to develop outside his center pawns, and starts
White's kingside assault.

(545)**** Swallow the bait!
1.Rxa6! willingly falling into the "trap" [1.a5 followed by b5
would be a more technically demanding way to win] **1...Bxd4
2.Rxf6 Bxf6.** But after **3.a5 Be5** [3...Bd8 4.Kd4] **4.b5 h4 5.a6**
the pawns cannot be stopped. (Alekhine – Bogoljubow, Dresden
1936)

(546)*** Beat the blockade
If White can achieve Nf1-d2-c4, blockading the center, then it
will be difficult for Black to make progress. Hence **1...c4! 2.bxc4
Ra3 3.Qd2 Qc5** (threatening d4-d3+) **4.Kg3 Bxc4.** Black has
regained the pawn, created a passed pawn, and opened lines
toward the White king. (Znosko-Borovsky – Alekhine, St.
Petersburg 1913)

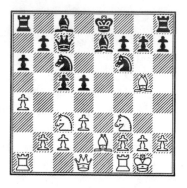

547. White to move

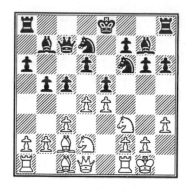

550. Black to move

548. Black to move

551. White to move

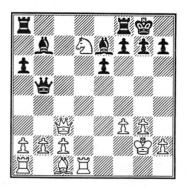

549. Black to move

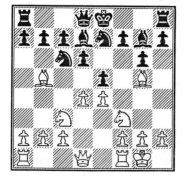

552. White to move

(547)* Remove the guard
1.Bxf6 Bxf6 2.Nxd5 wins a pawn.

(548)*** Resist the piece grab
1...b5?? traps the bishop, but loses material overall after 2.Bb6 Qe8 3.Nc7 Qd8 4.Nxa8 Qe8 5.Nc7 Qd8 6.Nd5 Qe8 7.Bc5. Better is **1...Nxd5 2.Qxd5 Ng4 3.Bg5 Qb6**.

(549)*** Swindle alert!
1...Qe2+ is the best move, but after **2.Kh3** Black must avoid 2...Qxd1?? 3.Bh6! losing his queen. Instead, **2...Bxf3!** forces White to give up his queen or be mated.

(550)** Pawn structure, piece activity
Generally, Black wouldn't want to "concede the center" by the pawn exchanges **1...cxd4 2.cxd4 exd4 3.Nxd4**. In this case, however, after **3...0–0 4.Re1 Rfe8** and **...Rac8** all of Black's pieces are wonderfully active, and e4 is a target. White has no way to attack the potentially weak d6 pawn.

(551)** Forks, rook on 7th rank
White wins the a5 pawn by **1.Na3! Ke7** [1...Kd7 2.Nc4 and the pawn cannot be defended: 2...a4 (2...Ra8 3.Nb6+) 3.Nb6+; 1...Bd3 2.Rc3 followed by Rc5] **2.Rc7+ Kf6 3.Ra7 Rc8 4.h3** and the pawn falls.

(552)*** Pins, remove the guard
By **1.Nd5!** White puts a severe strain on Black's position. The immediate threat is to capture at c6, when suddenly the e7 knight is inadequately defended. **1...Qc8** [1...h6 also falls short: 2.Bf6 Rh7 3.Bxc6 Bxc6 4.Bxe7 wins] **2.Nf6+ Bxf6** (otherwise White wins a piece by Nxd7 and d5) **3.Bxf6** with a clear advantage.

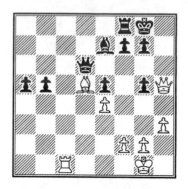

553. White to move

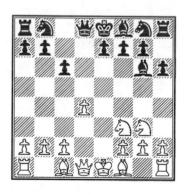

556. White to move

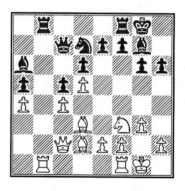

554. Black to move

557. Black to move

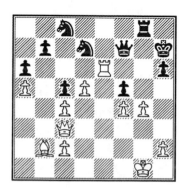

555. White to move

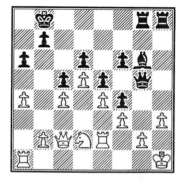

558. Black to move

(553)*** Take the perp
Down by two connected passed pawns, White has nothing better than the perpetual check **1.Rc6 Qa3 2.Rh6 gxh6 3.Qg6+ Kh8 4.Qxh6+** etc.

(554)*** Positional exchange sac
1...Rb4!! 2.Bxb4 cxb4. In return for the sacrificed material, Black gets a protected passed pawn, use of the c5 square, and potential presure against White's backward c-pawn. (Selezniev – Alekhine, Triberg 1921)

(555)** Final assault
1.Rxh6+! Kxh6 2.Qh3+ Kg6 [2...Qh5 3.Qxh5 mate] **3.Qh5** mate.

(556)*** Punish opening confusion
The opening moves were 1.e4 c6 2.d4 d5 3.Nc3 dxe4 4.Nxe4 Bf5 5.Ng3 Bg6 6.Nf3 h6?? (D). Black has confused two of the main lines of the Classical Caro-Kann: his last move would have been correct after 6.h4. Now from the diagrammed position White could have played **7.Ne5!** with a significant advantage, due to the softening of g6 and f7. The continuation might be **7...Bh7** [Black has a miserable structure after either 7...Qd6 8.Qg4 Nd7 9.Nxg6 Qxg6 10.Qxg6 fxg6 11.Bd3; or 7...Nf6 8.Nxg6 fxg6 9.Qd3] **8.Qf3 Nf6 9.Qb3** with a double attack on b7 and f7. In the actual game, White unfortunately played 7.h4??, transposing back to the book line and missing his chance.

(557)* Double attack
Black has mishandled this Exchange Grünfeld, putting his knight on c6 instead of challenging White's pawn center with ...c7-c5. He can redeem himself, however, by **1...Nxd4!** winning a pawn, e.g., **2.cxd4 Qxd4 3.Rb1 Qxc4.**

(558)*** Improve worst piece
1...Be8! is the way forward, intending ...Bd7 followed by a sacrifice on h3.

559. White to move

562. White to move

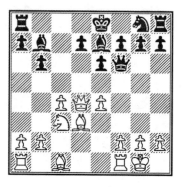

560. White to move

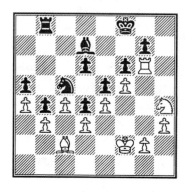

563. Black to move

561. White to move

564. White to move

(559)**** Active king

The White king would be unable to outflank Black's along the kingside. The best chance to win is to attack the queenside by **1.Kb4!** It looks as though White is marching into a brick wall, but in fact Black will be compelled to scuttle his d-pawn, or move (and thus weaken) his flank pawns. The finish could be **1...Kc6 2.Ka5! a6** [or 2...Kd6 3.Kb5 Kd7 4.Kc5 Kc6 5.b4 b6+ 6.Kc6 and Black pawns will drop] **3.b4 Kc7 4.b5 axb5 5.Kxb5 b6 6.Ka6! Kc6 7.a4! Kc7 8.Ka7! Kc6 9.Kb8! b5 10.a5! b4 11.a6 b3 12.a7 b2 13.a8Q+.** It is not possible or desirable to work out every possible line to the end – just see enough to pick the first move!

(560)** Seize weak square

The weakness of d6 points to **1.e5! Qh4 2.Qxh4 Bxh4 3.Nb5! Kf8 4.Nd6.**

(561)** One pawn stops two

1.b5! holds up Black's queenside pawn majority, enabling White to push his own pawns on the other flank.

(562)*** Create *luft* for king

1.h3!!. By giving his king air to breathe, White eliminates his back rank worries, allowing his rook to join in the assault [1.Bxf8?! Kxf8 and it's still a game] **1...Qxa3 2.Rd7 Qc1+ 3.Kf2!** [3.Kh2 Qf4+] **3...Qb2+ 4.Kg3 h5 5.Bxf8** and Black's defense crumbles.

(563)*** Piece sac for two passed pawns

With most of White's army on the kingside, Black should create queenside passed pawns by **1...Bxa4!! 2.bxa4 b3 3.Bb1 Nxa4 4.Nf3 Nc3 5.Nd2 a4.**

(564)** Discovered attack

White wins a piece with the discovered attack **1.Nd5! Qxd3 2.Nxe7+ Kh8 3.cxd3.** The knight is safe: it can emerge via c6 or be defended by Rb7.

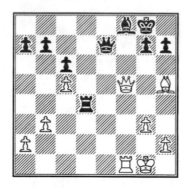

565. White to move

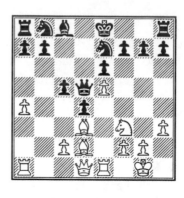

568. Black to move

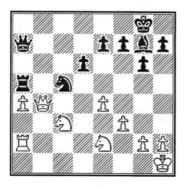

566. Black to move

569. Black to move

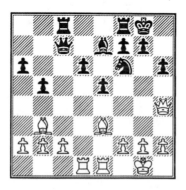

567. White to move

570. White to move

(565)*** Interference, weak back rank, discovered attack
White wins by **1.Bf7+! Kh8 2.Bd5!** (interfering with the Black rook's return to the 8th rank) **2...Rd1** [2...g6 3.Qxf8+ Qxf8 4.Rxf8+ Kg7 5.Rg8+ Kh6 6.Bc4; 2...h6 3.Qxf8+ Qxf8 4.Rxf8+ Kh7 5.Bf3] **3.Rxd1 g6 4.Qf2 cxd5 5.Qd4+ Bg7 6.Qxd5.**

(566)*** Double check
Black wins by **1...Nd3! 2.Qb3 Nf2+ 3.Kg1 Nxe4+** [the mating attempt 3...Nh3+?! intending 4.Kh1 Qg1+?? fails due to 5.Nxg1 Nf2+ 6.Rxf2] **4.Kh1 Nf2+ 5.Kg1 Bxc3 6.Nxc3 Nh3+ 7.Kf1 Qg1+ 8.Ke2 Qxg2+.** White's pawns will be decimated and his king remains exposed.

(567)** Destroy pawn cover
1.Bxh6! wins a vital pawn, since after **1...gxh6 2.Qxh6** there is no adequate defense against Re1-e3-g3 (or -h3).

(568)* Don't castle into attack
Black shouldn't even think about castling kingside at this moment – it's not worth the time to figure out whether the sacrifice Bxh7+ works (as a matter of fact, it does). It's better to get in **...Nbc6** and **...Ng6** first, while being wary of White's Be4 tricks.

(569)*** Don't allow perpetual check
With a dangerous passed pawn and heavy pressure on g2, Black should be pressing for a win. Thus **1...Kh5!** is called for, to reduce White's chances for perpetual check.

(570)**** Mating net, fork
1.a4+! Ka5 [1...Rxa4 2.Nc3+] **2.Nc5! b6** [now, conceding a pawn by 2...c6 is objectively best, as it is still a fight after 3.Nxb7+ Kb6 4.Nd6 Kc5] **3.c3!.** Suddenly the Black rook doesn't have many safe squares, and his king is caught in a mating net. Now **3...Rd2** [3...Rd5 4.Ka3 (threatening mate by b2-b4) 4...Rxc5 5.b4+; 3...Rd1 4.Kc4 bxc5 5.b4+ mating] **4.Ka3!** forces Black to give up his rook to stop b2-b4 mate.

571. White to move

574. White to move

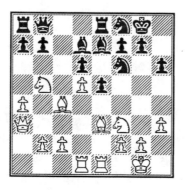

572. Black to move

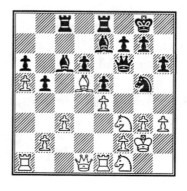

575. White to move

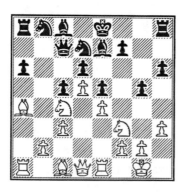

573. White to move

576. White to move

(571)**** Sac, sac, mate!
1.Bxh7+!! Kxh7 [1...Kh8 2.Qh5 and there's no defense against Bg6+] **2.Qh5+ Kg8 3.Bf6!**. White forces mate, e.g., **3...Re6** [3...gxf6 4.exf6 with Qg5+ and mate next] **4.Qg5 Rxf6 5.exf6 g6 6.Qh6** then Qg7 mate.

(572)** Double attack, discovered attack
1...a6! wins material: **2.Nc3** [2.Na7 Rxa7 3.Bxa7 Qxa7] **2...b5 3.Be2** [3.axb5 axb5 attacking a3 and c4] **3...b4** with a pawn fork.

(573)*** Fork, central breakthrough
1.Nfxe5! dxe5 2.d6 Bxd6 3.Nxd6+. White enjoys a lead in development, a much safer king, and the superior pawn structure. One possibility now is **3...Ke7 4.Qd5 Qxd6 5.Qxa8** winning the exchange.

(574)*** Defend loose piece
Black's threat is 1...Bxd4 2.Bxd4 Rxc3! 3.Rxc3 Rxe2 nabbing two minor pieces for a rook. White played 1.Rfd1 and met with 1...Rxe3! 2.fxe3 Qe7 3.Na2 Rxc1 4.Nxc1 Bxa4 5.Qxa4 Qxe3+ 6.Kh1 when 6...Bxd4 would have been excellent for Black. A better defense is **1.Rfe1** or **1.Bd3**. (Lautier – Topalov, Elista 1988)

(575)** Superior minor piece
White is left with the superior minor piece after **1.Nxg5 Qxg5 2.Bxc6 Rxc6 3.Ne3** followed by **Nd5**.

(576)*** Sac pawn to get rook on 7th rank
Black has a number of weak pawns, but White needs a way to get to them: **1.e4!** [1.f5 exf5 2.Rxd5 Rd8 3.Rxf5 also wins] with the idea **1...dxe4 2.Rd7 Rb8 3.Kf2**. White will regain the material with interest. In the game Black declined the pawn offer but resigned after 1...Rd8 2.exd5 exd5 3.Re1 Kf8 4.Bd4 Ra8 5.c6! Nd8 [5...bxc6 6.Bc5+ Kg8 7.Re6 Nd8 8.Re8+ Kf7 9.Rh8 h6 10.Bb6] 6.Bc5+ Kg8 7.Re8+. (Alekhine – Euwe, Amsterdam 1937)

577. White to move

580. White to move

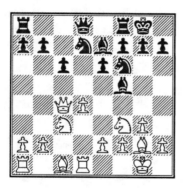

578. Black to move

581. White to move

579. White to move

582. Black to move

(577)** Cut off opponent's king
1.Rd6!, cutting off the Black king's approach toward e2, is the only winning move. **1...Kb5 2.Kd4 Ka5 3.Kc5 Ka4 4.Kc6**, etc.

(578)** Trapped piece
1...Bc2! wins the exchange, for if the rook moves, then ...Nb6 traps the White queen. (Csom – Lukács, Budapest 1979)

(579)** Mating attack
1.g4!. Black must part with his queen to prevent mate: **1...Qxe6 2.Rxe6**.

(580)*** Decoy, blunder check
The immediate Nxf6 would uncover a fierce attack on g6, but unfortunately this loses to ...Qxg3. On the other hand, if Nxf6 could be achieved with check, then this idea might work. Thus **1.Rh7+!!** Kxh7 [or 1...Kf8 2.Qxg6 Ke8 3.Nc5! mating shortly] **2.Nxf6+ Nxf6 3.Qxg6+ Kh8 4.Rh1+** with mate to follow.

(581)**** Overworked piece, pin, attack
1.Ne5!. The Black queen is now overworked, having to guard both d7 and f6. This enables White to double the Black f-pawn (or ruin the pawn cover in some other way), opening lines to the Black king. For example: **1...Nxe5** [1...Bc8 2.Ng4! Nxd4 3.Nxf6+ gxf6 4.Bh4 Nf5 5.Bxf5 exf5 6.Nxd5 with a crushing attack; 1...h6 2.Bxf6 gxf6 (2...Qxf6 3.Nxd7) 3.Qg4+ Kh8 4.Qh5 Kg7 5.Re3 with a deadly check to follow; 1...Kh8 2.Bxf6 gxf6 3.Qh5 f5 4.Nxf7+ winning the queen; 1...Nxd4 2.Nxd7 Qxd7 3.Bxf6 gxf6 4.Qg4+ bagging a piece] **2.dxe5 h6 3.exf6 hxg5 4.Qh5** mate to follow.

(582)** Discovered attack
Black wins a pawn by **1...exd4 2.Nxd4** [2.Bxf6 Bxf6 doesn't help White] **2...Nxe4! 3.Nxe4** [3.Bxe7 Qxe7 is no better] **3...Bxg5**.

206

583. White to move

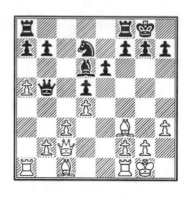

586. Black to move

584. White to move

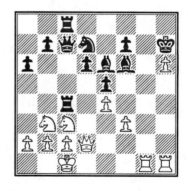

587. White to move

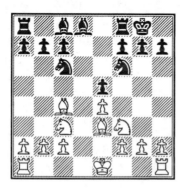

585. White to move

588. Black to move

(583)*** Pin, weak back rank
1.h3! eliminates White's back rank weakness, thus activating the threat of Rxe1. If the queen escapes, unpinning the White rook, then Black's back rank issues come into play [1.Qf8+?? Rxf8 and now White's rook is pinned, making Rxf8 (mate) impossible; 1.Rxe1?? loses to 1...Rxe1+] **1...Qe2** [1...Qe7 2.Qxe7] **2.Qf8+** with mate to follow.

(584)** Fade-away jumper
1.Ne1!. There is no defense against Nd3, winning at least the exchange.

(585)** Induce weaknesses
1.Bc5! Re8 [1...Bc7 loses a pawn: 2.Bxc7 Nxc7 3.Nxc5] **2.Ng5 Be6** (the only way to defend f7) **3.Nxe6 fxe6 4.Bb5** followed by Bxc6. Black is left with two pairs of doubled isolated pawns. (Vasiukov – Gheorghiu, Manila 1974)

(586)* Deflection
1...Bh2+! 2.Kxh2 Qxf1 wins the exchange.

(587)*** There's a right way and a wrong way
It would be a mistake to assume that Black will fall for 1.Rg7+ Bxg7?? 2.hxg7+ Kxg7 [2...Kg8 3.Rh8+ Kxg7 4.Qh6 mate; 2...Kg6 3.Qh6 mate] 3.Qh6+ Kg8 4.Qh8 mate. Of course, Black need not be so cooperative. After 1...Kh8 2.Qg2 Qd8 White is a piece down without a clear win. Rather, White should play **1.Qg2!** forcing mate, e.g., **1...Rxc3 2.Qg7+ Bxg7 3.hxg7+ Kg8 4.Rh8** mate. (Adorjan – Ribli, Budapest 1979)

(588)*** Prevent unfavorable exchange
The knight on c7 is helping to hold off White's minority attack, which is based on a3-a4 followed by b4-b5. Therefore Black plays **1...Bd6!** to prevent its exchange. There followed **2.Bxd6 Nb5 3.Qb3 Nxd6** and Black has further improved the position of his knight. (Portisch – Kasparov, Skelleftea 1989)

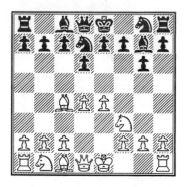

589. White to move

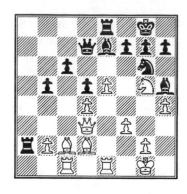

592. White to move

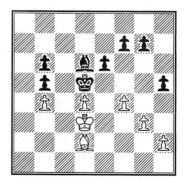

590. Black to move

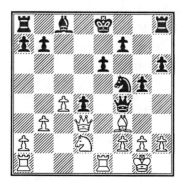

593. White to move

591. White to move

594. Black to move

(589)*** Fork, trapped piece, mate
1.Bxf7+! Kf8 is utterly miserable for Black [1...Kxf7 2.Ng5+ Ke8 (2...Kf8 3.Nc6+; 2...Kf6 3.Qf3 mate) 3.Nc6 smothers the Black queen]. (Ibragimov – Zhelnin, Moscow 1998)

(590)**** Induce weakness, *zugzwang*
White is already tied down to the defense of b4 and d4. **1...h4!!** induces yet another weakness at f4. Otherwise White can block the position by h4. **2.gxh4** [or 2.Bc3 g5!, for example, 3.fxg5 (3.gxh4 gxh4 4.Bd2 h3 and because White's bishop is already busy guarding b4 and f4, his king must give way and allow Black's king into c4 or c4) 3...Bxg3! with the idea 4.hxg3 h3] **2...g6 3.h3 f5** White is in *zugzwang*, and must shed pawns.

(591)** The tactic fails
1.Qf3 Qe8 2.Re1 maintains White's advantage. White must not try to win the exchange by 1.Nf7+?? Rxf7 2.Bxf7 since Black then has 2...Qe7 winning back a whole piece.

(592)*** The tactic fails, interference
1.g4? traps and wins the bishop, but at too high a price: 1...Bxg4 2.fxg4 Qxg4+ 3.Kf1 Qxh4. Black has three pawns for the piece, and the White king remains vulnerable. White should first play **1.e6!** which compels a Black pawn to block his own queen. **1...fxe6 2.g4 Bxg4 3.fxg4**.

(593)* Pin, remove the guard
1.g3 removes the guard of the knight on f5 (note that the c6 pawn is pinned).

(594)*** King position, skewer
1...Kg2!! wins, and is the only move that doesn't lose [1...Kxh2? 2.Ke4 Kg2 3.Ke3 and Black loses his pawn]. **2.h4 Kxf2 3.h5 Ke2 4.h6 f2 5.h7 f1Q 6.h8Q Qa1+** skewers the enemy royalty.

595. White to move

598. White to move

596. White to move

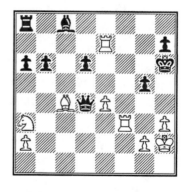

599. White to move

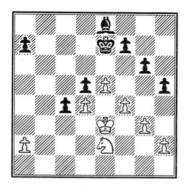

597. White to move

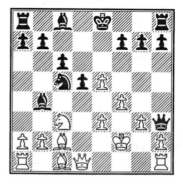

600. Black to move

(595)** Promotion, skewer
1.Rh8! wins, as **1...Rxc7 2.Rxh7+** skewers the rook.

(596)*** Create passed pawns
1.f5!! Kd7 [1...gxf5 2.g6 and the g-pawn is unstoppable; 1...fxg5 2.fxg6] **2.fxg6 Ke8 3.gxf6 exf6 4.Kd5 Ke7 5.c4**. White will create another passed pawn on the queenside.

(597)**** Make knight superior to bishop
With so many Black pawns on the same color as the bishop, White has the potentially superior minor piece. White must now create an outpost for his knight and work to make that placement advantageous. **1.f5!**. White begins to fight for the f4 square for his knight. **1...g5** [on 1...gxf5 2.Nf4 Bc6 3.Nxh5 White's outside passed pawn assures victory] **2.h4! f6** [2...gxh4 3.gxh4 gives White f4 without a fight] **3.hxg5! fxg5 4.Ng1!** Now the threat is 5.Nh3 g4 6.Nf4. **4...Bd7 5.f6+ Ke8 6.Nf3 g4 7.Nh4 Be6 8.Ng6 Bf7 9.Nf4** (mission accomplished; now e5-e6 is in the air) **9...Kd7 10.Kd2**. Black soon ran out of safe moves and had to abandon pawns. (Alekhine – Yates, Hastings 1925)

(598)** Pin, double attack
1.Re1! picks off a bishop: **1...Be6** [1...Bd8 2.Re8; 1...Bf8 2.Re8] **2.f5**.

(599)** Interference, mating net
1.e5! interferes with the Black queen's coverage of f6. Now Black must pitch his queen to stop Rf6+ followed by mate.

(600)*** Superior minor piece
1...Bxc3 2.bxc3 Bf5 3.Bxf5 Qxf5. The Black knight will dominate from e4. (Makagonov – Botvinnik, Sverdlovsk 1943)

Acknowledgements

It is my privilege to thank IM John Watson for providing advice and encouragement throughout this project, making numerous suggestions for improving the manuscript, and kindly writing the Foreword. I am grateful to NM Dan Heisman for helping me to understand the importance of the *thought process* in chess. My thanks also to IM Igor Khmelnitsky, Charles A. Temple, and Bob Long, who generously furnished helpful comments. I am indebted to Lori Sellstrom, my editor, and Atilla Vekony, Publishing Information Manager at Wheatmark; it was a joy to work with them. Finally, let me tender my appreciation to the House of Staunton (www.houseofstaunton.com), for the use of their Capablanca Series chess set in the cover design.

R.C.
June 2007

Printed in the United States
102048LV00002B/181-189/A